PRAISE FOR CALLING ALL POETS

"In the two decades in which I've been a CAPS fan, I have been wowed time and again by the poets and the poetry of my beloved Hudson Valley. What you hold in your hands is but the tip of a glorious iceberg, but what a refreshing tip it is!"

~ John Leonard Pielmeier, actor, poet, playwright (Agnes of God, The Boys of Winter, Hook's Tale, The Exorcist); novelist, (Hook's Tale); screenwriter (The Pillars of The Earth)

"This anthology captures the vital community of writers living in the Hudson Valley. Calling All Poets over the course of twenty years as evidenced in this volume has nurtured and supported numerous poets, with distinct voices, approaches, styles, and genres. This is a rich and compelling collection of works that speaks deeply to many aspects of the human experience and provides illumination; childhood memories, family relationships, lost love, the search for the meaning in existence, and the witnessing of injustice are all powerfully portrayed. I appreciate the range of form and style from lyric poems to personal and prose poetry, from rich descriptive sensory pieces to philosophical inquiries and surreal and mythic visions. This is a volume that deserves to be read many times, and each time a reader will find new poetic treasures."

Jan Zlotnik Schmidt, SUNY Distinguished Teaching Professor
co-editor of A Slant of Light: Contemporary Women Writers of the Hudson Valley

"Calling All Poets has successfully created a diverse community of poets and writers who support one another. Whenever I'm there, I feel as if I am part of something bigger, a movement in the arts. In addition, they have embraced technology, streaming readers outside the area live and broadcasting the events online. Calling all Poets is the best series in the Hudson Valley!"

~ Rebecca Schumejda, poet
Cadillac Men, Waiting at the Dead End Diner

"The Hudson Valley boasts a plethora of fascinating poets whose active participation in readings and local events makes them a reliable source of wisdom and inspiration."

~ Dr. Lucia Cherciu, poet
Lepădarea de Limbă (The Abandonment of Language)

"The Hudson Valley gives voice to writers and poets who have something of value to say and a comfortable environment for accomplishing this important endeavor. From the caves of Rosendale to the richness of Roost Studios, the Hudson Valley has nurtured me and advanced my career."

~ Eddie Bell, author, poet
Capt's Dreaming Chair, Festival of Tears

CAPS Poetry
25th Anniversary
Anthology

CAPS Poetry 25th Anniversary Anthology

Edited by CAPS Editorial Board

CAPS Poetry 25th Anniversary
CAPS Poetry © 2024 by Calling All Poets, Inc., 501(c)(3)
All Rights Reserved
No part of this publication may be reproduced, distributed, or transmitted in any form or by any means, including photocopying, recording, or other electronic or mechanical methods, without the prior written permission of the publisher, except in the case of brief quotations embodied in critical reviews and certain other noncommercial uses permitted by copyright law. For permission requests, write to the publishers, addressed "Attention: Permissions" at info@callingallpoets.net.

callingallpoets.net

ISBN   978-0-9973258-7-4

Published by CAPS Press
Authors of individual works retain all rights
to the poems in this anthology.

Current Venue of Calling All Poets Series

Unison
9 Paradies Lane
New Paltz, NY 12561

Book design: small packages, inc.
Cover art: Greg Correll

dedicated to you

CONTENTS

Title	Page	Author
Improvisation	1	Roger Aplon
Ukraine 2022	2	Roger Aplon
Elegy for a 20-Year Marriage: Anniversary	4	Catherine Arra
Tilling The Serenity Prayer	5	Arthur Devya
Buried in Leaves	7	Amy Barone
Volcán Tenorio	8	John Bartell
Look down at coyotes with me	9	Rachel Baum
The Water	10	Eddie Bell
The Unfree	11	Eddie Bell
the shape of wind	12	Naomi Bindman
Chris had no idea	14	Mark Blackford
The Country Neighbor	15	Marianna Boncek
Kintsugi	16	Kim Brandon
Transient	17	Ron Bremner
It was clear	18	Tim Brennan
Notes From a Terrestrial 3rd Place	19	Tim Brennan
Cape Cod	20	Penny Brodie
All Old Friends	21	Daniel Brown
The Door Wall	22	David Capellaro
Nature Boy (inspired by Nat King Cole)	23	Patricia Carragon
Half Awake and Dreaming Finalist	24	Alan Catlin
Elegy for the First Snow of the Season	25	Dr. Lucia Cherciu
Saunter at Sunup	26	Dr. Lucia Cherciu
Invasion of the body Ukraine 1st Place	27	Susan Chute
Breakers	29	Samul Claiborne
My Grandfather d.	31	Cassandra d. Clarke
Swamp Red Maple	32	Paul Clemente
Dance of Life	33	Chris Collins

Title	Page	Author
Amythic	34	Jack Cooper
Passing Time	35	Teresa Costa
Location Science	36	Ruth Danon
Grief	37	Ruth Danon
Evening Prayer	38	Joann Deiudicibus
Apalachicola	39	Lenny DellaRocca
The Invention of Horses	40	Lenny DellaRocca
To Trust the Light	41	Deborah DeNicola
From Inside the Ring	42	Deborah DeNicola
Sleeping Tips for the Partially Blind	43	John Dorsey
Poem After Listening to Philip Levine	44	John Dorsey
Coronavirus	45	Gina R. Evers
Coronavirus	46	Gina R. Evers
Finding the Car	47	Karen Fabiane
2 Cherita for Leonard Cohen	48	Sharon Ferrante
A Diorama for Judith	49	Thomas Festa
No Picture Survives of Memory Jones	50	Mark Fogarty
Behind the Veil	51	Poet Gold
The Weight of Thoughts	52	Shotsie Gorman
Around The Corner	53	Roberta Gould
After The Ice Storm	54	Carol Graser
That Winter	56	Carol Graser
plume	57	Meghan Grupposo
Kitchen Rules	58	Maggie Hall
Absence of Birds	59	Janet Hamill
Ascension	60	Anthony Howarth
Philaster, Keats & the way of Bushido	61	Matthew Hupert
Exodus	62	Kate Hymes
Listening to Music from "The Thief of Baghdad"	66	Sharon Israel
Hurricane	67	Kitty Jospe
Duplex thinking of all those fallen in war, fallen prey to accidents, fallen prey to bad circumstances, fallen and unable to rise	68	Kitty Jospe

Mother Nature Has Her Way	69	Mary Louise Kiernan
A Poetry Reading in Bushwick	70	Ron Kolm
Patricide	71	Susan Konz
To See Like James Clerk Maxwell*	72	Darcie Kortan
Jackie 1 1966 silver silk screen print, Andy Warhol	74	Raphael Kosek
Grandma's Honey Cake	75	Don Krieger
Memorial Day, 2019	76	Don Krieger
iPhone	77	Katherine Latella
On Days Like This	79	Bonnie Law
Sphere	80	David Lawton
Daughters of Destiny	82	Rain Lee
Rivers and Gardens	83	Phillip X Levine
Friday The 13th	86	Heller Levinsom
Interlude in the Garage	87	Maria Lisella
A Gift of Hammers…	88	Maria Lisella
Noise -for Samantha-	90	Brian Liston
Red-eyed on the Red-eye	91	Timothy Liu
Bela and the Rats	93	Julie Lomoe
Core Value	95	Phil Lynch
A Voice in The Produce Aisle	96	Betty MacDonald
Drive	97	Mary Makofske
The Door Rattles When She Steps In	99	John Martucci
Public Safety Announcement	100	Prince McNally
The Shift Forman's Daughter	101	Tana Miller
Halloween Leafage	103	Ermira Mitre
Memorabilia	104	Beth SK Morris
to that child hiding in the bomb shelter	105	K.R. Morrison
Rainbow, A Week After Going to the Photoville Festival 2023 Brooklyn Bridge Park, NY	106	Karen Neuberg
Like a hand reaching out	107	Mary Newell
Seventy and Counting	108	Perry S. Nicholas
Dear Dear Han Shan	109	Will Nixon

Lucy	110	John O'Conner
Gnomen	112	Irene O'Garden
Again & Again, the Berkshires	113	Michael O'Mara
Late Fall Sunset	115	Mary K O'Melveny
October	116	Kathy Poppino
...despite the omission from the contents page I am documented in every cell of ontological being	117	Siobhan Potter
Sight	118	Linette Rabsatt
November 2020 (a Thanksgiving pantoum) inspired by Joy Harjo's 'Perhaps the world ends here'	119	Carrie Magness Radner
ordinarily, she marched — Uvalde	120	Suzanne S. Rancourt
gift of moon she clenched with teeth	121	Suzanne S. Rancourt
Feathers	122	Guy Reed
Warp and Weft	124	Liz Reilly
Strikes	125	Donna Reis
White Crosses	126	Sally Rhoades
Black Moth	128	Cheryl A. Rice
An Interruption	130	Stephen Roberts
Sweet	131	Heather Christy Robinson
In Your Sleep	132	Tom Romeo
Shelling the Peas for my grandmother	133	Amanda Russell
single-room oratorio, summer	134	Stephanie JT Russell
Done In	136	Stephanie JT Russell
Desired, or Not	137	Margaret R. Sáraco
Winterscape	138	Judith Saunders
For My Father: The Cartographer	139	**Jan Schmidt**
One Among Many	140	Moe Seager
The heron's in the dirty pond again,	142	William Seaton
Breath of Spring, June 2023	143	Jim Seegert
Invisible Burqa	145	Debbie Shave
Just This One	148	Nancy Shih-Knodel
Beautiful Ripples —for Roberto Burl Marx	149	Gary Siegel

Grandma dreams	150	Nathan Smith
The Beautiful Death Around Us	152	Megha Sood
Yesterday	153	Amanda Spadafino
Red Button	154	Matthew J, Spireng
Predator	155	Lisa St. John
Liminal Life	156	Victoria Sullivan
All Wars Are The Same	157	Victoria Sullivan
The History of Jazz	159	Tim Tomlinson
Adolescents of 1968	160	Tim Tomlinson
Word play	161	Daniel Villegas
The Next Time I Fall In Love	164	George Wallace
The Object Of My Desire	165	George Wallace
Convalescence	166	Bruce Weber
it was just another weekend in 1885 for mick	167	Bruce Weber
John Lennon	168	Dan Wilcox
The Glass Studio	169	Sandra Yannone
The Brotherhood of Sleeping Car Porters	170	Sandra Yannone
Concrete Ekphrasis	173	Glenn Werner

IN MEMORIAM

Bluejay	176	Bob Barci
Untitled	178	Saul Bennett
Rain Walk	180	Barbara Boncek
Street Blues	182	Frank Boyer
The Secret	183	Frank Boyer
Lillith	185	Enid Dame
In the Garden of the Senior Residence	186	Lew Gardner
A Villanelle for Kathryn, The Pilot's Wife	189	Lynn Hoines
Crucifiction	191	Lei Issac
A Disturbance In Thr Crowd	193	Donald Lev
Uncovered	194	Shirley Powell

The Cave	197	Pamela Twining
Elements of Style	199	Pauline Uchmanowicz
The Green Piano: I —for Bill Heine	201	Janine Pommy Vega
Shofar	203	Ron Dionysius Whiteurs
...	205	Don Yacullo

CAPS BOARD MEMBERS

6 Haiku	229	Mike Jurkovic
title here	230	Jim Eve
Punchline	231	Ken Holland
Your Mouth	232	Greg Correll

"Poetry is not only a dream and vision;
it is the skeleton architecture of our lives.
It lays the foundations for a future of change,
a bridge across our fears of what has never been before."

Audre Lorde

"A poet's work is to name the unnamable, to point at frauds,
to take sides, start arguments, shape the world,
and stop it going to sleep."

Salman Rushdie

"Poetry lifts the veil from
the hidden beauty of the world, and
makes familiar objects be as if they were not familiar."

Percy Bysshe Shelley

PREFACES

What can I say about CAPS that all of you have not said in one way, shape, or form over these last 25 years? Those here, those missing, those who have joined the journey and moved on...

Together we've recorded a history that has created a unique bond. Our thriving and robust community has a universal language that transcends its Hudson Valley roots and now welcomes voices from around the world. It is a language we engage fully with and embark willfully upon.

I know for me, CAPS has kept me honest. We are here by design, providence, or delirious adventure. And we are here now.

~ Mike Jurkovic
Producer and Host, CAPS Jazzoetry at Quinn's and PPD
Producer and C0-Host, the Calling All Poets Series

What was a simple thought put into action twenty-five years ago and enacted without a clear vision, is now an acknowledge literary engine promoting written and spoken word works, events, as well as poets and writers throughout the Hudson Valley and beyond. I started CAPS as it's known as a simple poetry reading at the Howland Cultural Center in Beacon New York because I enjoyed poetry and the camaraderie of the poets who willingly shared their works with an audience. I never envisioned it to be what it is today. A streaming venue on the internet and via YouTube featuring poets throughout the Hudson Valley, the Tri-State area and internationally. There are so many to thank for helping to bring CAPS to where it is today. So I start by thanking all our members and those who have participated and support CAPS throughout these twenty five years. Too many to lists here, but valued by all of us here at Calling All Poets. To Mike Jurkovic and Greg Correll thank you for bringing this program to the heights it is now, a place I could not imagine twenty-five years ago.

~ Jim Eve
Founder and Co-Host, the Calling All Poets Series

I made all the usual mistakes when I first started to read my work. Not looking at the audience, mumbling in a monotone, afraid to emote. I got impatient, waiting to read, and was anxious to leave when I was done.

Great writing penetrated, though. Took me out of myself, inspired me, set a bar for my own poetry. Over the years, listening at CAPS, all writing began to matter, because I learned to listen on more than one level. To hear what was intended, not just the attempt.

I was too critical, and worked on my half-assed Buddhism.

In Ben Lerner's The Hatred of Poetry, he explains the inevitable failure of all poets, all poetry, to meet expectations. And how to change expectations, go deeper.

I learned to respect, to love, anyone brave enough to scribble lines, much less stand and read—and I learned this at CAPS. To love the effort and feeling, whether the craft was there or not. To admire the craft, when the heart of a poem was obscured. To feel ecstatic when a poet's work contained everything: polish and ability, original choices, ineffable soul.

And to expect the sublime from CAPS poets.

~ Greg Correll
CUNY Writers Institute Fellow

INTRODUCTION

A word about our winners and anthology finalists.

We hardly need call out that all such judgments are highly subjective. Every poem included in the anthology by default merited (and received) consideration. So every poet is, in a sense, a winner, with or without any official designation. In support of this comment, we want to note that our original intention was to select three poems as our first, second, and third place winners…along with a cash award. While that still held fast, it was the quality of the overall submissions that led us to create a list of twelve finalists in addition to our three winners—finalists whose work we felt worthy of an extra level of attention.

Please know that all poems received multiple readings, and the readings were judged blind. We were both impressed and pleased to have read poems of great diversity. It's a testament and a reflection of the CAPS reading series, both now and certainly into the future.

CAPS congratulates the following poets and their poems as our award winners:

    First Place: Susan Chute, "Invasion of the Body Ukraine"
    Second Place: Sandra Yannone, "The Glass Studio"
    Third Place: Timothy Brennan, "Notes From a Terrestrial"

And to our finalists, in alphabetical order:

    Alan Caitlan, "Half Awake and Dreaming"
    Ruth Danon, "Grief"
    John Dorsey, "Sleeping Tips for the Partially Blind"
    Gina R. Evers,
        "Coronavirus (after reading Natalie Diaz's The Facts of Art)"
    Meghan Grupposo, "Plume"
    Matthew Hupert, "Philaster, Keats, & the way of Bushido"
    Bonnie Law, "On Days Like This"
    Heller Levinson, "Friday the 13th"
    Mary Makofske, "Drive"
    Karen Neuberg, "In"
    Tim Tomlinson, "The History of Jazz"
    Glenn Werner, "25 Wide Pantoum"

The three winning poems and the finalists' poems appear in the body of the anthology.

We want to again thank every contributor. It's our privilege to publish your work.

~ Ken Holland
February 2024

The Poems

Improvisation
After Charles Lloyd's Collection "8" Part 5
Ruminations

Roger Aplon

First   There was the passion   That   Inquisitive   Anxious   Tormented   Sensation   Haunted   By time   That intimate intruder   Whispering in his ear   Listen   You'll Soon   Hear him   Succumb   One light touch   Gives way   Sways in & over   The puzzle expands   Listen   You'll find him   Poking around   Under the covers   Between the ever-light   Opposing the dark   Phrase by Phrase   &   One   After Another . . .   There's no time to salvage   Memory   Each sweep   Every stroke   Each riff   Blind to prediction   The bag of possibilities has been rendered   &   The fires are lit   Hear them out back   Banging their applause   Yes   One goes his way &   There are those to hold his coat   The next   Drives   Out of the circle   & still   The triangle pops   &   bops . . . there's a secret   Enfolding   As if   /   As if   He's known it all along   & here we are   Messing with his Musings . . . Come on . . .   You're not alone   The extraordinary   expands   Up the mountain   To the peak   Tap-Tap   &   Rat-a-tat-tat   &   Crash   &   Crush   &   Tic-Tic-Tic   &   Charles tempts   &   Charles taunts   &   tickles   &   flows   &   . . .   &   The keys intercede   &   through it all   Calm as butter   Slippery as a cloud   He Ruminates, Reconciles   &   Recollects   As Testy   &   As Tasty as Time   Alone

Ukraine 2022

Roger Aplon

It begins with a question

What is it
eviscerates morality,
invites the birth of a beast where a taxi-driver, plumber or
an accountant, once lived
a humane life?

**

The first one was a young boy. The doctors registered him as Unknown
No.1
Time Magazine – When War Comes Home

*

I'm here. Room 32.
I've removed the shrapnel from his chest & legs & arms & now
I insert a breathing tube & crank up the machine
to do the work.

I've been here thirty-six hours & am headed home to the subway
where my mother & sister crouch among their slim necessities:
paper to clean ourselves, water, toothbrush,
blanket.

"I'm here too," says my daughter. Now six, she has a doll, pink shoes, a
Minnie Mouse barrette & a CD player that's run out of juice.
She hopes for a night,
when she can dream of summer.

**

I'm an anonymous soldier. Before, I was a candy maker.
Today, we lifted an old man across the gap to the arms of his shuddering wife
of fifty years. They carried bread
& a bible.

I've shot men & watched them die. Once our brother Slavs, they've come
to war & worse: they've slaughtered our innocents, stacked them
like cordwood,
left us

the vacant stares of women raped by squads of men,
left us babies
decapitated & strung like gourds from street-signs &
lampposts...

*

Our killer's corpses lay stiff
& broken,
in the ditches.
Once
husbands, fathers, sons & lovers – like us . . . Just
like us...

*

Who can say

What it is
eviscerates morality,
invites the birth of a beast where a taxi-driver, plumber or
an accountant, once lived
a humane life?

Elegy for a Twenty-Year Marriage: Anniversary

Catherine Arra

She catches the scent of Giorgio cologne,
the timbre of his baritone.

Laughter, locked in stairways of the home
they shared, moans at night.

A teddy bear birthday gift
sits still and silent on the rocker.

The ghost of her lingers too long in the past
when she prefers to walk rigorous miles

or settle with Mala beads to count 108 breaths
for each white jade and bodhi seed orb

or make music thunder, and dance
because she loves to dance

or talk to animals and birds,
deadlift 100 pounds at the gym.

Today she counts dogwood blossoms as they loosen
and fall from the tree they planted and married under.

In a few days, the counting will end.
She will give the tree to the woods.

Tilling The Serenity Prayer

Arthur Devya

"Grant me the serenity."
Can I ask for that?
My peace is buried under experience and questions.
It is a thing that disappears when I look directly,
and reveals itself when I turn away.
Like a hand gentle on my shoulder,
from somewhere a whisper
"to grant yourself serenity – yes."

The violence, the misunderstanding,
I cannot alter what took place.
Or the mistakes I made
three days ago when I said those things.
The DNA that makes me seem different to you.
And how hard the world shakes
something so fragile it breaks.
There is no stopping the declaration of my body,
growing up, growing old.
These things shriek at me until
I "accept the things I cannot change"
and I become the rock in the stream,
steadfast while the rapids flow by.

Reaching deep, can I conjure
the courage to change my ways?
Take hold with both hands
my hunger, relentless, demonic,
And bring it up close to my face.
To stop my own noise and really hear
what you are saying to me.
How much bravery do I need
to voice dissent, start a new politic?
To show myself with all my odd shapes and colors.
With slow steps I descend into the cave
to find a diamond made from unbearable pressure.

It is the "courage to change the things I can."

When I have done a little thing,
that small effort, even though it is
only a half turn of the screw,
it is some movement to see.
A small blossom of knowing buds.
I learn the difference between
how much to water the delicate plant
and when to let the sun help it grow.
It is then, I feel I have taken a breath of
"wisdom to know the difference."

Buried in Leaves

Amy Barone

Autumn in childhood
recalls sheltering trees.

Vibrant hues and trudging hums
through crisp fallen leaves.

Big future plans brewed,
as we headed to the 5 & 10
for our vice—fistfuls of candy.

A friend's older sister blasted
Tommy, a rock opera from The Who
that scared me; I preferred Motown
and the Monkees' bubblegum pop.

Long before family wars, broken vows,
and mislaid dreams joined piles of leaves.

Volcán Tenorio

John Bartell

I don't know if you're aware,
but there's a tapir in our backyard,
and a buff-throated saltator
sitting in a cedarwood.

The woman with the French eyes
is chasing the tapir
in the rain,
hoping for that one good shot,
the one she'll show her friends
as they sip wine.

There are flies in the jam and
banaquits out front,
poking their beaks wherever they can.

It's raining.
Again.
My shoes are soaked
and my clothes will never dry.

There's a tapir in our backyard,
and it seems very content,
edging into the brush,
disappearance,
as if it never existed,
like a petal dropped into the wind,
a contrail fading in a far-off sky.

Look down at coyotes with me

Rachel Baum

My hands shake, spilling tangerine IPA,
pale orange liquid overflowing a plastic
cup, you say that hiding behind a door
or a tree is futile, and I don't want to
believe it because when you are unmoored,
you need a wharf or a pier, not more ocean.

The wild-eyed coyotes focus on the curl
of foam, the receding wave that is me,
they spring from their haunches, chase
through thick water into the worst
part of night, their swimming pool jaws
snap, they aim for my throat, ready to swill
bloody mouthwash.

Look down, you can hear them panting,
a rock concert of tumbling, careening sound.
Perch on this scaffolding with me, look down,
see what I see, how the crowd swirls,
how tattooed fans morph into burnished
coyote fur, then the short bristled hair,
the dander, the tidy, clipped nails of dogs,
the dog, the one that waits, like death, for me.

The Water
(After visiting the Legacy Museum Montgomery, AL)

Eddie Bell

It was the water, tumbling, rolling, agitated water
The water had me, tossed me aboard the ship
Against my will like the souls to which I lay chained
I could feel it slap against the ship's weathered lumber
The water. The water.
So real. So frightening. So unknown
My sickened mind and body revolted against the dark
The smell
The moans
What was this thing?
My fear bristled. I shook. I cried
The gods abandoned me to hell
I felt the terror and shit upon myself

It was too real this entrance to the Legacy Museum
That repository of truths
I struggled back to reality as the surrounding water sounded seasick waves
My mind said this was too much and I should leave
But pressed on I did
Walked past the scattered sculpted heads
My ancestors' portraits in the sands
Taken by the imagery of the punishment iron
born around their blood drenched necks
I cringed; the torture all too real

But it was the water, tumbling, angry that holds me still
The water. The water.
The terrifying water and the graves that it holds.

The Unfree

Eddie Bell

Sea waters lapped the shore
ancestors' shackles in-place heavy laden
their ship docks at Godsden's wharf

Shuffler shuffle clank clank
putrid fear sickness-bound sea to dungeon
their journey's end enslavement

Cotton rice indigo tobacco cane
enslavers riches wrought from unfree souls
whipped starved buried replaced.

the shape of wind

Naomi Bindman

close enough to kiss
two hawks pass, coiling
in air, enraptured raptors
eyes catching pieces of light
radical pairs quantumly entangled
Earth's magnetic field flashing
below like runway beacons
visible pathways guiding their flight,
do they also see the gusts
on which they glide, currents
curling under their wings
a deep greyblue sea, or
tornado of green, fiery flames
surging with the wind's pulse
sparks swirling like starry skies,
tidal waves of wind crashing
over houses, howling sirens
of windsong rattling windows,
washing through trees swaying
languidly like old lovers dancing,
the hush of leaves shushing,
pouring through wild fields of
tall grasses rushing, swells and
eddies and pools, lakes of wind
thin trickles, swirling tentacles
of wind like writhing snakes,
fingers of wind beckoning,
tendrils twirling like smoke,
ribbons of air tying bows in
twisting strands of hair, brushing
ripples across reed shades, sending
shivers over the surface of a stream
or licking sun-bare skin,

the shape of dunes of sand,
scalloped edges of drifted snow,
rain slicing sheets, sheets billowing
on a line like puffs of clouds, fluffs of
down floating upward, dandelion tufts
like snowflakes blowing sideways
in gyrating arabesques, leftover luffs
of sails, or spinnakers filled round
like Dizzy's cheeks, a pirouetting
dancer, an ice skater spinning
faster and faster, a dervish whirling,
fluttering of prayer flags and butterfly
wings, an escaped balloon ascending
slowly spiraling up and up and up
perhaps to heaven, breezes cascading
unendingly around this tiny blue jewel,
the shape of earth's breath, birdsong,
the shape of a poem flowing, of petals
opening, of undulating saplings their
silver backs of leaves shining like new
flowers, wild rose perfume rising,
the shape of chimes singing, a sigh,
a whisper, a laugh wafting, the breath
of a beloved caressing, the shape of love.

Chris had no idea

Mark Blackford

the heroin contained fentanyl.
It's impossible to tell without trying.
That's the appeal of the cut junk. That gambler's high:
The excitement
of rolling your dice across a puddle rife with unknowns, going
all-in against a House that eventually always
wins.
He knew that part, too well.

The Country Neighbor

Marianna Boncek

The morning of my mother's funeral
the humidity finally broke.
The sun rose a friendly yellow
as if the heatwave of the last few days
had just been a petulant child's temper.
I knew the farm hands
must be on their second breakfast
when he appeared at the funeral parlor door
his tie crooked as he slipped on his jacket.
He approached my mother's coffin,
bowed his head but did not kneel.
I watched him as he turned looking for me.
He approached,
put his calloused hand on my shoulder.
"Sorry to hear about your ma," he said.
I nodded, accepting what he had to give.
Then he said, "I gotta run.
You know how it is, gotta get the hay in
before the next round of storms."
He left, already pulling off the tie and jacket in the parking lot,
I knew he would lead the farm hands
as they worked cutting and baling,
in a few verses
of Amazing Grace.

Kintsugi

Kim Brandon

When you were gone
That first night alone swallowed joy
Spit out the vision of a sweet tomorrow

Like the emperors tea pot shattered
The heart fell to the floor broken

A low song of sorrow humming at dawn
A black swan floats on the edge of despair

To keep vigil for twenty seven sunsets for your love to return
The ripped paper sonnets gave way to the lingering salty kisses of loss

It was only when the tea steeped to perfection was poured
An extended hand steady with compassion

Offers a hot sip of a new season
The tea pot of you repaired by minutes gone by

The bright gold inlays boldly holding together
A stronger heart where imperfections

That masquerade as loneliness
Give way to the enduring yet forgetful strength

Of readying the heart to love another again
When life caresses, shakes, and trembles us so.

Transient

Ron Bremner

With your transient greygreen eyes, you try to decipher a pathway to glory, knowing its fleeting fame will not subsidize your sorrow, nor buttress the pillars of your whims. You float above all this realtime circumstance, hoping that the ephemeral will save you. But like the ducks below, you know you'll have to jump into the pond with the rest of the least eventually. You fervently wish that the water will cool you when you're too hot to go on with your sundry lives.

It was clear
      (roughly after Carl Phillips', For Night to Fall)

Tim Brennan

IT WAS CLEAR from the start that hours had slipped
past the shoreline. The trees sensed a change
in the frangible air and drew coins
from their pockets,
for there's always a cost to these things,
which calls to mind
what I've given to sun-burnt beggars
in my stingiest moments––
blips I would rather not share.

Each moment stands like a precipice from which I peer,
goaded toward then recoiling from
the open air, the vacant end
of a future quivering above the forest below
which asks for a name to put
to the face with the questioning look.

Notes From a Terrestrial

3rd Place

Tim Brennan

Crossing the estuary by foot, a messiah stumbled,
fell and drowned. The sea grass moaned. Gulls
refused to eat, spurning boats that returned
with fresh-caught lamprey straining in the nets.
Architects whose visions could only
have been built with slave labor, jumped
from cliffs pounding their breasts.
And, the organ grinder, whose children run
foreign corporations, raised his schnapps with glass
fingers, to toast another pretender.

In earlier times, emperors spoke
with tongues of stone cut for their temples.
Then tourists and the reporters arrived.
The awakened subjects soon refused to kneel
and, to the casual refrain in an old song,
were muscled off to unknown locations.

Tonight, as we celebrate the moon
and its confederation of satellite states
with cocktails and thawing shrimp at the bar,
men in dark ties and ankle sensors surround us,
asking for names and phone numbers. Then
they force-feed us extended warrantees
high in wood pulp impossible to digest.

Cape Cod

Penny Brodie

Wispy white clouds
Salty foaming waves
Indefinite forms brushed by ocean winds,
Drawn by lunar tides.

From shore to horizon to heaven above
Water reflects sweeping blues of sky,
Tiny mirrors blink from pools at low tide
Warmer shallow waves wrap around sandy feet,
Combing for shells or a pretty rock
Nature's treasures, turning dull later,
Upon a shelf, mantel or dresser top.

A reminder of where they came from
Of where you have been
Waiting to glisten again,
At home, in the sea.

All Old Friends

Daniel Brown

One is a Librarian dying of cancer
arranging daily bouquets, while others
prattle on about temporary weather,
another a man who understands
the mystery of grief
watching a boat
at dawn with only a running light
shining into fog,
a woman who sees paradise
in the dust of the street,
a young housewife compared to a leaf,
Langston's centuries of rivers,
Rilke's blind and beggars,
Blake's smiles of love and deceit
and chartered London streets.

Several more. All old friends I embrace
in turn at regular meetings,
after the internet tumult of
yellow and red autumn poems like leaves
cover me in a pixelated wind,
and I feel the sorrow of lack of time to
view these strangers as I
would want them to view me,
before they take their place on the hustling street
bumping and jostling me along,
such singular faces they have hurrying past
each beautiful in their own way,
as I stare over their heads looking for
a familiar hand above the throng.

The Door Wall

David Capellaro

I hear the doors–
Some with glass,
Most just solid wood,
All fixed into a backyard fence and weathered.
Cockeyed door panels
Bound in chronograms of overlaid paint colors
Silhouette their ghosted stanchions' shapes,
While shades of time
Silently whisper through door knob holes and key slots,
Bearing secrets
That very few,
If any,
Still hold.

Nature Boy
    (inspired by Nat King Cole)

Patricia Carragon

I was told that a silent space
existed within us,
even for fools and kings—
a secret chamber
where pain found love
for healing to begin.

No reservations,
boarding passes, passports,
luggage, wardrobes, or currency
required.

No need for photos, postcards,
or souvenirs
to mark one's journey.

No walls for seclusion—
emptiness was impervious
and aware of interruption.

I took that journey,
let Zen take my hand,
walked into emptiness
where love sat in the corner—
her head and heart
between her legs.

Half Awake and Dreaming

Finalist

Alan Catlin

1-

Like a deKoonig woman:
daubs of gray and red and blue,

a yellow hat with green feathers,
a dream book in her hands.

2-

Time lapse photos of the moon
cycling through phases:
waxing, waning, going dark;
coronas of available light.

3-

Ghost images trapped in
a scaling mirror; all of them
struggling to get out.

4-

Ghost light on bare stage,
empty seats and the exit
signs glare; wild shadows scatter.

5-

Dry ice filling orchestra pit,
simulating an Arctic plain;
frozen music.

6-

After the chiming of the hour,
restive shadows retreat;
time crystalized.

Elegy for the First Snow of the Season

Dr. Lucia Cherciu

The cat sits on my lap. I dream of cardamom,
hand-knit wool socks, and cathedrals. Mother, I wish

I had listened and stayed home. A woman
with red hair wears a bright green scarf.

To all the women who live far from their mothers,
I say, buy several bags of haloes and give them

to your elderly neighbors. Give them walnuts, almonds,
and fresh raspberries for the heart. This season

is time to convince an old man to give up
his car keys. Promise you will stop by

to listen to his stories once a week. Promise
you will give him a ride to his friends.

Intractable, refractory, obstreperous.
Recalcitrant, recusant, contrary:

time to let go. Leave the road to others
to bend their cars on the guardrails.

Leave the guilt to others to shapeshift
from bragging to complaining.

Leave the posturing to others to obviate
the need for alms, good deeds, old stories.

Saunter at Sunup

Dr. Lucia Cherciu

Your eyes are a river where I bathe every morning
in the shade of a willow tree in the village

where I was born. I am not afraid. I do not doubt.
I know you are there. Your eyes are a river

of fishes that never run out, generosity that never
exhausts itself, abundance of laughter and listening.

Your eyes are a river of dance. I walked
the neighborhood of your kindness.

Who bathes in the river of your salt and sugar?
Who steals mock orange for you? Who labels

the pots when planting stone pits for plum trees
and loses them, so when the tendrils of a small tree

arrive, it's hard to tell what it was? Who believes
in you, coaxes the day out of shadows, unmoors

someone who's lost? Who escapes the unrelenting
pressure of showing? Drenched in perfume,

the sunset. Steeped in music, the stroll.

Invasion of the body Ukraine1st Place

Susan Chute

1

A curtain of darkness dresses us,
necklaced with pinprick leaks of light.

A shadow is a baseless lamp
A suitcase is a wing on the ground

The cough is a violet exposé
to be tossed in the trash

My skin separates
the darkness without and within

The infection of invasion
is just a matter of time

2

In distant lands
from rockets placed or misplaced

> The woman stares, arms akimbo
> The smoke from the guns
> is bluer than honesty
> blue as inkstain on silk
> Blue as ash in the fireplace
> ember dying out
> This is the block that hides heaven
> This is the block that hides hell

Citizens cower in subways
A bunch of rags is a woman crying
The darkness swallows the throat
Hunger is the opposite of an orchid's tongue

Stop the trains the planes expel the diplomats
tear up the monopoly money drain the vodka
What can you do to stop a war without warring

3

I am a country cut off
from casualties and curses of powerful pariahs
cut off from consequence

Of course the books will bury us
Of course the breath is a stop sign
Of course the choke will stall
Of course the solemn is statement

    If I call, you will be occupied
    If I'm not in sight, I will forget
    If I remember, the surprise will sharpen me
    If I trust you, my heart will race
    If I imagine my death, I will die
    If I sleep, will I awaken

    If I tell the truth, will I understand the ending

A pregnant woman runs
A cigarette is a rubbled street
forming a wall that doesn't stop anything

They said the bugs crawled through me
but I am out of the weapon's range

Breakers

Samul Claiborne

I smelled your breakers curling over me
As I flew waist deep in your surge
Lips blue and body unwilling to leave

Music echoed in your rolling shell
Old tinny songs flowing from the beating
Of stranded kelp against the taut skins
Of empty ray and skate eggs

Victrolas and daguerreotypes
Impossibly old things
Crowded my young mind
As I tumbled round your streaming

I traded freedom for symbiosis
Breath for timelessness
Warmth and equilibrium
For merging with your motion
As you bowled me down into the rasping shoal
And diced me on your coral bridges

And as I lay back flat and silent
On sand bar's bottom
Watching your scintillic dance
Swaying above me
You held me beneath
To last breath
Releasing me finally
To sound surface for air

You never cared
Only played
You never noticed
Only held me in negligent caress
And pounded me with careless blows

Yet you were all I was meant to see
All I was meant to breathe
Until you cast me
Weak kneed and wobbly
Up on the stony break
And willed the sun to warm me once more

My Grandfather d.

Cassandra D. Clarke

I did not understand your powers
that you were a threat
When you would only speak of questions,
when it was close to death
I did not understand at the moment,
the transfer of part of your spirit and what it was telling me

That I must find out, the rest
My hug agreed that I had to do my best
I did not understand that my DNA would frighten me,
as I looked at the test
I did not understand the Native inside of me
Or Abraham's request
I did not understand!

Swamp Red Maple

Paul Clemente

You cannot trust a swamp red maple
to give you sugar and warming wood.
Her sap's too thin to be a staple.
Her brittle boughs misunderstood.

Although her limbs expect decay,
a learned tree knows angry wails
and fights the Fall's fiercest display.
She spurns the reaper and the gales.

October masts fly scarlet jibs.
In the breeze, a hush, a chime,
for branches weak as children's ribs
that fail when on their windswept climb

and do not return to reproduce.
So thoroughly are the prunings shed
that dawn reveals a somber truce
to let the living collect the dead.

You cannot trust a swamp red maple
to supply your sugar and warming wood.
Her sap's too thin to be a staple.
Her brittle boughs misunderstood.

Dance of Life

Chris Collins

two trunks rise above the tall
forest trees
limbs stretched wide –
a fierce giant standing
stone-steady on solid ground –
in a posture of defense
to battle the wailing winds
of hurricane force that
tear break and topple
such spartan beasts

below those pine titans is the
small fragile gram-weighted worm
that plods dumb on soil
without the armor of bark – bulk –
height – heft – dense trunk – deep
roots and long limbs
but survives natural forces
with pliant softness using its
internal bristles to reach out
grasp the soil and anchor itself
quietly riding out any storm

of all nature's creatures both
large and small
none is superior to the other
each is endowed and
specially designed to survive
the dance of life together

Amythic

Jack Cooper

Sometimes there can be no Agamemnon,
nor Clytemnestra.

Things must remain as they are:
the tiny, troubled souls

unknown to any but themselves.
There, beneath the moment,

abridged, the interval that lingers
like breath, we take what solace avails

disappointment, errors leading to mistake
suddenly realized if uncomprehended.

Give us this day wholly to make
amends for all had not been

anticipated, the slippage that lands
only precisely when we fall.

Passing Time

Teresa Costa

The mouth
defecates
a world
starved
of love.
Unreasonable
speeds
dominate
reformed
inhabitants.
The need to
catch up
is silver
platters of
time
handed
multi-dimensionally.
The soul
screams for
placement
of
passions
grown.
It's no wonder
Time passes us
by with
second thoughts.

Location Science

Ruth Danon

I locate myself in the neighborhood
of cats. There are only two of them
so it's a pretty small place. There's
one of me most of the time except
when the other human appears. It's
a quiet neighborhood; a lot of time
we are asleep. We like sleeping and
also eating. We always eat together
though we don't eat the same food.
The cats sit on the table. At times
one paw or another stretches
towards the salmon on the table.
Salmon is very pretty to look at,
pink on its plate, almost the color
of the cat's tongue. Neither paw
nor mouth ever reach salmon;
gesture more hypothesis than
reality, a manifestation of desire,
as if the cat is acting out what
I feel. I, of course, eat the fish,
bathed in lemon and capers.
Lately I've had cooking on
my mind as well as cats. I like
sleeping as much as they do.
One cat demands to look at
himself in the bathroom mirror.
He looks at himself and is
always bewildered. I stand by
him, also bewildered by the self
I see in front of me. Who is
this person, so small now, so
diminished, altered, lonely,
singular and quiet in this
now fully fallen world?

Grief   **Finalist**

Ruth Danon

So much spread out   early evening
      fog over the mountain, hardly
a mountain you would say,
      aching for the west, but
not kidding yourself about that
      dead man found on
the bench above Pocatello,
      a place you love
so much   and we are
      so tired after so much
weather, in an exhausted time,
      so much time to take
in so much.   all worth naming:
flood and fire, hail
      dropping, the sound
unfamiliar as your
      growing anxiety, which is not
unfounded,   enough
      to make a person go unhinged
as though doors and
      floors were falling away
galaxies fleeing
      all the objects once
held so close drifting
      through space
and reassembling somewhere
      as if the universe of what was
once your life is no
      more than a cabinet of curiosities
      "look," we say, "at that one and that
one and that one. . ."

Evening Prayer

Joann Deiudicibus

A girl with a broken arm in flight
swings wingless in a dream
after fighting the fall to sleep.
In a screen-blue room
she exhales the day, drowsy
beneath a cool sheet of shadows.

A once-feral cat from Bronx streets
toys with a mouse, leaps and lands.
Chasing a tired tail, she tucks herself
down until lids play hide-and-peek.
She'll stay for now,
as long as her nature allows.

Once the windows shut their eyes,
the devoted return, leave
the hours behind. The air
moves over them, purified—spell-
slipped, all, into the listening dark.

Night—give dark cover to the dozing
stray and her solitary kitten; to some-
one else's daughter in my bed.
Keep them hidden till day.
Let rest what will rise with the light.

Apalachicola

Lenny DellaRocca

Laughing gulls whirl and scream before they spiral down
to a thousand
oyster shells
along the river
bank where I stand
photographing
some old fish house
wrecked and leaning
hard to ground. Rusted
corrugated pieces of
metal swing in the wind
sounding like
mechanical men
whose last breaths
bang loud
beautiful goodbyes.
Crows look at me from
dead lights inside the hulk before taking to the sky
in black streaks,
winged alphabet
only they and the gulls
understand. Then
something glitters
in the weeds, but it's not
too bright, a dull spoon
perhaps, flung I suppose
by a boy in a passing car
weeks back or years,
hard to say. Because
the sun makes much
of little things
that can take its shine
and throw it back
like a crashed
star or what's left of a tin can on a southern afternoon.

Note: a Laughing gull is a species of sea gull

The Invention of Horses

Lenny DellaRocca

Lynda Hull shines in the cafe with her syringe. Sits across
from me
at a table
where lovers
gouged their names
with the history
of cigarettes.
She wipes sugar
to the floor.
Each grain
a lonely beatnik.
This is a dream
I say to myself.
She says
All beautiful
creatures come
out of the past,
from a fever, come galloping through our souls like prayers.
I tell her that
I don't believe
in prayer.
I say, You make
black mares out
of coffee cups.
And just then
our server drops
her grandmother's
earring. It's a swift
ride that almost
wakes me. The
spinning quick
of it tells a story.
In the flickering
light of its wonderful
fall are stallions and the bright women who tamed them.

To Trust the Light

Deborah DeNicola

You must let the Light seduce you.
You've no reason to resist. Yet you will—
insist, that is—you'll want to know

the all of it, will not commit to less.
You want commitment to the Self
that spent her life beneath the sun. Baked

from outside in, skin humming like an engine—
You want to drive it, dominate it. You want it to obey.
Until then, you can rationalize away

the way burnt stars leave only trails of flint.
But even scant light hints at brighter gifts.
A sidelong flash may turn your head,

though you won't claim it. Someday,
you'll wish you hadn't been
the undiluted absolutist, and still the Light

will chase you down the street.
It's shining through your sleep.
Too long you've held to doubts,

facets of Truth, pigment
prisms to protect you, glowing
stones like geomancers use—

Maybe on your death bed, maybe then
you'll chant I do—there are more
reasons here than answers.

The body runs on light.
and when it's finally shed—
That glittering dawn of dust

is sustenance, it must
go somewhere else,
go on—.

From Inside the Ring

Deborah DeNicola

You want circumference in birdsong this morning.
To lie in the light of the window and focus
on surround sound as a picture draws itself
within your head. You want a visual sketch
of mutual notes, synesthesia played by a harp-
shaped robin, or an alto parrot with talent for the violin.

Silly, you admit, but here you are in the antique
iron bed with books about France all around you.
Half-opened, bookmarked, and lines quoted on
post-its. You want the Languedoc tongue,
newly-invented vowels, a rotunda of open-armed
sound in a circle—In the wreath of a spotlight
projected on stage, you want an orchestra
warming up. You'll wear that cloud
of distortion like fantasy fur, a halo of hair.

It's your mouth surprised into kissing, the flutter
of arms over a loved one's neck. It's the lake
where you skate, your synapse and sensor, your
central electric, where you circle yourself into center,
the brew and the bubbles you generate. It's where

you find wholeness in myth, the glow
of the pacing you stumble around in.
Where you aim to end up, or begin,
the home of all wonderment.

Sleeping Tips for the Partially Blind   **Finalist**

John Dorsey

after they check your blood pressure
you mention again how you can't sleep
& the nurse reminds you
that you have only one eye now
as if you could ever forget
she says that the blind
sometimes have trouble sleeping
& that might be your problem too
you think about light you don't notice now
things in dreams that just feel incomplete
like an unfinished painting
or half of a song
where you never get to see
how lovely a girl's hands are
when there are only half as many stars
to radiate the night sky.

Poem After Listening to Philip Levine

John Dorsey

after this
everything becomes a grease stain
in a field of tired hands
caught in the rain
where the paradise of youth
just boxes you in
until you can't breathe
you lick memories from your fingers
to fill your stomach in the late afternoon
until the blood from a day's work tastes like honey
until flowers that should be sweet
just seem flawed
& that's exactly
what you like about them.

Coronavirus 1

Gina R. Evers

For six weeks, aerosol disinfectant
has been out of stock. I want it for

the mattresses. My Gram would mist her bedspread
every morning: scent of sterility —

our new safety — in her sheets. I woke early,
was to lie still until little hand

reached the eight. Also on her dresser:
a framed portrait of Jesus, his sacred heart,

cosmetic mirror, gray-blue canister
of Lysol. All neatly atop white lace

handkerchiefs. An altar.
The doors in her room — one to the attic, one closet, one

the exit — seemed, to me, mouths of monsters
turned on their sides. But a grandmother's bed

has always been the safest place to be,
and lucky, when she's sleeping beside you.

When it's time to wake — magic of Sunday sun
surging past curtains still being drawn,

glittering dust in the air; it dances.
Her touch enchants blankets as they billow,

one at a time, perfect arcs above her bed.
And finally, that sacred spray

catches light, turns the whole room to color.

I can still smell the meal that comes next:
cinnamon raisin toast, with warm butter.

Coronavirus
After reading Natalie Diaz's "The Facts of Art"

Finalist

Gina R. Evers

On NPR, I listen to the refrigerated trucks
parked at the curbs of New York City hospitals.

Poised to carry bodies no different
than the bones of Native babies

uncovered from the mesa
when Southwestern highways needed to be cut.

"Hopi men and women—brown, and small, and claylike ...
the silvered bones glinting from the freshly sliced dirt-and-rock wall—"

The virus is better
because it understands

no human life is worth more than another.

How is it then
that box trucks fill with our elders,

our brown-skinned beauties,
my students' tias and abuelitas?

I isolate at home, 90-miles north.
I listen. I write. I answer the phone

when a friend from the Midwest calls to say,
"I am sending you some sage."

Finding the Car

Karen Fabiane

Walking ahead, almost
marching. Nearly vocational
your path energized by a resolve
I'd maybe reconcile
later.
Postscript

to a communal gallery reading, episodes
of people within
& outside too, as Fridays become; so many
galvanized
with work gone for the week; bosses' blames deleted,
 just dropped,
& then the night too. Celebratory secretions
exhausted, trying
to revive every dead part of you, but remaining
almost lock-
step. Done. Recent events
discarded like music played, fading
untouched.

Busy avenue a memory receiving sleepwalkers, hookers on a last
go-round, rummies
in doorways, & the car (almost
where we left it) long ago;
retrieved. Found
blocks from the park, in a neighborhood 1 of us
nearly dwelt
during a previous bout of sentience. Trying
to reanimate the dead. Too late

to revive the living.

2 Cherita for Leonard Cohen

Sharon Ferrante

in a foggy room

with a fine-tuned horn
on a legendary lap

he finds
the answer
to the mysteries

below the tower

a monk
gives away his cloak

all
that matters
is the heart

A Diorama for Judith

Thomas Festa

I was looking at two elephants
on the savannah, one little and one grown.

With their fabled memory, their tools,
their songs, death rituals, and art.

It seemed trees everywhere were changing.
How could the alder shine so bright

against the backdrop churn
of dark storm clouds?

Autumn had just begun,
the smell of solvent strong,

lights running along the tunnel's length.
It was all an anachronism, time's charade—

the photo an oasis, a memory-pool.
Under glass at a redbrick hotel in Richmond,

capital of a country that never was, you held
your cast above night-lit water like a trunk,

the swimming pool jade as a polished bookend.
These were the seasons of our life together,

high-gloss pages casually flipped through,
tall pampas grass swaying as we trampled past.

I look out and see a stone bridge
framed by branches heavy with the setting sun

and think how I snorkeled up
the mud pool so you could drink.

No Picture Survives of Memory Jones

Mark Fogarty

Nothing of Memory Jones survived the fire.
If a photo was taken in her two years on earth
It vanished with her and her parents.
The Times said she enjoyed gospel music
And hanging with her mother when she made food.

My student's mother lives in an SRO.
I've seen a picture. It looks as grim
As a debtor's prison. She has a hospital bed
And a second bed for her homeless daughter
For the nights she wants a place to sleep
Or something to eat if there's any food there.

Her daughter was in the room the night the place caught fire.
She carried her mother out of the burning building.

May her memory be a blessing and carry her forth

Behind the Veil

Poet Gold

There are Mirrors

                Doors

                            Layers

reflections of our lives
bits and pieces
thoughts
silenced
turned into rumbles
mini quakes
deep in the soul
hidden behind the veil

There's so much to say.

Prolonged whispers
like wind in the night
we can't ignore
deafening
cracking the landscape

Behind the veil
no one notices but you

                Complicit

                        in one's own absence

words

we never dare speak
become descending tears
seeping into the corners of our mouths
leaving crystals on our tongue
tiny little cubes perhaps abandoned
dissolved or
transformed

The Weight of Thoughts

Shotsie Gorman

Woolen thoughts.
Warmest when no one knows.

 Like, when they're asleep,
for instance, and you drape them,
in two blue blankets.

You are not concerned with yourself.
Your thoughts are weightless.
Less than your deeds,
As it should be.
Your arms are cold as well.

It's when they don't know
It's from you.
Whoever you are.

 Weightless, selfless.
You sit there,
knowing, they'll live past
your time

 So sweetly sad, you know,
That's the rub
like, blue wool.

Around The Corner

Roberta Gould

When the streets changed names
I kept on
Imagined forever
delighting
The trees waited
their flowers proceeded
burgeoning or dropping
petals aged the night before.

I sat down, let them continue
without looking
My gaze might harm them
I'm from a difficult species

When I stood up
they were still there!
The street was a carpet
strewn violet and rose
My feet were delighted
Despite their shoes

After The Ice Storm

Carol Graser

When the tree falls on your car and you've
known the tree for 22 years, it's trunk and height

it's cedar bright smell, it's branches that once
held your bantam rooster crowing at 4 AM

while you flung shoes at its cocky dim shape
that kept the snow off the bottom corner

of the driveway and hid the house enough
from the busy road. The car too you've known

for 80,000 miles, the car that made
the long commute almost bearable

that came to you after your father died
your father who had two accidents

in two years in the new car he bought after
your mother died, the second accident

happening during a mini stroke that didn't
kill him but led to a mysterious decline

that led you to ask the doctors to stop
trying, and the money your father left

made you think to buy a new used car and
here was this Prius at the dealer priced

unusually low for a two-year-old car
with 9,000 miles but it had been in two

accidents with its previous owner who,
you imagine, was in their 80's like your

father, crashing their last car, so the car is
family and the tree and they've both gone

together. Maybe you'll plant a lilac
bush in its place at the driveway's end

and there will be a new car and it will always
be the car you got after the one you

got because your father died, the one that
was smushed end to end by the trunk

of the old, cherished tree and you'll say,

Remember the tall tree, the fuel-efficient car
the father whose love was a pine needle smack.

Remember the tall tree, the fuel-efficient car
the father whose love was a pine needle drink

Remember the tall tree, the fuel-efficient car
the father whose love was a pine needle drink

That Winter

Carol Graser

After the long snowmelt
the ground froze and we walked
over the brown grass like
cement, unforgiving

and the moon rose like
a full radiant pearl
that melted nothing. We sat
all in our separate chairs

and told our disparate
stories. The wind repeated
herself: cold & cold
& cold & cold. We blinked

against frosted cheeks. Some
of us knew the story
that would call a softer
wind. They were still cradling

its newness. They were still
nursing its hunger. What could
we do but wait, let our breath
warm our frigid fingers

plume   Finalist

Meghan Grupposo

call from a distant tree
rouse & stir

I descend stairs
moonless sky
   unlocks the door

listen:
clicking claws on
   clay shingles

kinetic display
a calling train, I'm

partial to your peacock cry

rustle, rattle
trill, set
alight, alight

      be smoke

Kitchen Rules

Maggie Hall

I don't live in a house anymore; they took my keys and changed the door. Going to sleep thinking of tomorrow; wrapped in plastic skin, caught up in a loop of black rope; remembering to go to chemist and replace the drugs. Wear the red dress you picked up from the post-office; no make-up is required as you'll be wearing a mask. Don't forget that I like my furniture to come with instructions.

When you're playing the Sub and feeling the Dom; I didn't give you permission to leave. She looks beautiful as the shape of words form in her mouth; dry lips wetted as the sea kisses salt. Backstage there is a room marked by a star; tonight, it's ladies' night for the officers at the burlesque hall. In Christian theology those who remain shall be saved; don't stop being witness to the remnants let in DNA. Coding paint and sculpting air-dried clay the dark wind opens his mouth to the sun while translating Beowulf riddles, I turn into a song.

Cherry picking stones picked up by the queen; David Bowie in a collar of white horses, dressed in a blue planet wearing black stilettos. I sent the email a question mark carved out of the dead spine of a ripped corset; scrolling the dream with electric sheep I look up to see my name carved into the pupils. The mattress has broken springs and squeaks on every turn; Ophelia wrapped up in chains as she floats in a plastic wedding dress, where loneliness falls away into two versions of the same dream.

The painting of a boy and his basket of fruit; Perseus under the protection of Zeus; trapped in a bag of snake heads there is a red crotchet playing her song. Freemason dancing with a wolf; all through the night copyright dreaming with the light on; cracking shells into the sun, have you noticed there is an AI companion option on ZOOM?

Present your balls I'm going to use the whip; now gently touch my feet; next read to me a random selection of books, preferably something about how to cook. You took too long to come when I called, so there will be no worship for a month. I have added 5- lashes of the crop to each ball. She keeps an owl in her pocket to chase photons in the background of a carefully staged room; the record player's needle scratches over dusty recordings playing a grand mal seizure fugue in F sharp minor.

Absence of Birds

Janet Hamill

Almost a total absence of birds
in winter the woods were forsaken
where Florence Street came to an end
a network frozen of ponds & bare trees

In winter the woods were forsaken
doing figure eights on antique blades
a network of frozen ponds & bare trees
singing Chattanooga Choo Choo

Doing figure eights on antique blades
made before filming Sun Valley Serenade
singing Chattanooga Choo Choo
all by myself   in immaculate silence

Made before filming Sun Valley Serenade
I was training for the Winter Olympics
all by myself   in immaculate silence
almost a total absence of birds

Anthony Howarth

ASCENSION
for Philippe Petit

                                    hallelujah
                                    an echoing
                                    his arms extended
                                    earth and heaven
                                    floor and ceiling
                                    his bridge between
                                    at the top he stands
                                    stares in disbelief
                                    and the congregation
                                    as the piano plays below
                                    inch by inch
                                    forward and upward
                                    slides his body
                                    round the cable
                                    wraps his big toe
he's arrested   a perch above the altar
   because   it reaches
      important people   extend it until
         don't want a circus   at the cathedral door
            in their beautiful   an inch-thick wire
               church   anchor
                  but a priest   lets him
                     intervenes

Philaster, Keats & the way of Bushido   **Finalist**

Matthew Hupert

Make a cup of my skull like the Buddhists do in Lhasa
Bang my bones like a xylophone or giant Taiko drum from Kyoto
      hewn from a single piece of Keyaki tree stained the color of
bleeding
Play my poems on a standing bell or singing bowl
      to echo & fade in diminuendo off high sky peaks through verdant
valleys
All things are writ on water
My name is writ on water
Water someday sipped from a silent pool after dripping
from leaves golden or green

Exodus

Kate Hymes

October 16, 1777. Then the enemy under the command of General Henry Clinton and General Vaughan came to Kingston in Esopus, and burnt my dwelling-house, barn, cider- house or storehouse, and another barn and wagon house at my late dwelling house, and also a small out-kitchen which was left standing when my dwelling house was burnt down the 23rd of October, 1776. And the enemy burnt all the houses, barns (except one house and barn) in the town, church and county house, likewise laid everything in rubbish of ashes-fences and everything they came to. And they carried away with them one negro man named Harry, two negro wenches, jenny and Flora, and destroyed all my household goods and furniture and my library of books.

—Journal of Col. Abraham Hasrouck

I.

The Storm

No need to stir these dying coals
to spark another day's cook fire.
Nobody here but us, Harry, Jenny
and me. They call me Flora.

As soon as the alarm sounded the whole of
Kingston town was in a tizzy. They carried off
cattle, sheep, and hogs, loaded chickens and
ducks into crates. The Mister and Missus
packed their best frocks, precious stones
and gold pieces sewn into hems and waistbands.
They ran away with everything valued.

I lay beside smoldering embers
In dirt on the verge of a hard freeze.
I keep my eyes shut against the first crack
of dawn. I dream:

I am a rush of storm
waters, once green leaves
churn in my foam. I breach
creek banks as I run through
the woods. My torrent wears down
boulders and stones in my way. I rampage
onward – one insignificant stream
joins up with another and another. We become
a raging cascade
        all the way down the Esopus,
        all the way down the Roundout,
all the way down to the river,
out to the sea and open waters
that carry us home.

The earth I lay upon shudders
and rumbles. I feel the march of
freedom on Its way. This is the day.
I open my eyes to witness
a sky aglow with deliverance.

II.

The Fire

My work is to keep the fires
burning. I am the first line of defense
against winter's march down from
the mountains into the valley,
the frost strips trees naked. I chop
away limbs from trunks, set them aside
for a season of seasoning
until ready to be hauled into
a stone house, stacked in a corner waiting
to be called into service. Old Man Abram
and his sons are keepers of the kindling,

the spark that ignites a flame. They dole
out dry twig by twig. Guess they afraid
I might build a fire hot enough to chase
them out of the house and into hellfire.

The old man and his sons sit as close
to the heat as they can stand. The news
coming upriver makes them shiver. They talk
as they always do as if I was a log
stacked in the corner without eyes to see
or ears to hear. Unseen, I move
among them keeping their cider cups
warm and full. I wait for the heat to rise
in their bellies and set their tongues loose.
Their voices rise as logs flare and sparks fly
Up the chimney. A knot in the wood pops,
shoots embers at their feet, and onto
the parchment they hold so dear –
they call it a declaration. Swear upon it as though
it is a holy book -- they swear to die
as free men than live in servitude to a man
faraway across the sea. Abraham calls me:

> Harry,
> get my boys their guns. They're
> going off to fight for liberty.

I am a man. I am the fire.

III.

Oya

They call me Jenny.
The ladies say I am their best girl,
menfolk call me wench. York's
boy says he calls himself Aganjú. He says
my true name is Oya. Our home, Guinea land,

is faraway across the sea where the kingdom
streets are paved with gold.

In the orchard
where we meet, he tells me
I am the brilliance of
an October sunset. The sky glows
the colors of flame in my presence. When I am
with him, I am full of spirit and heat. I am not
best girl, I am not wench. I am beloved.
I am Oya, river goddess. I command
lightning and wind and thunderbolts.

We lay atop a golden and fiery
bed, watch stars shoot and streak
across the blackness above our heads.
Aganjú says only pale ghosts fear
darkness. Night covers us. We bare
our souls and tell our truths.

He tells me:

>   I plan to run. The British say
>   they will set free men who fight
>   these would be masters
>   of the world. Don't cry. I will come back.
>   When the alarm sounds,
>   look for me. I will be at the head
>   of the march, a north star
>   pointing the way to Kingston town.

Listening to Music from "The Thief of Baghdad"

Sharon Israel

The earth's geography always seemed
so flat to me. But now, topography,
suddenly alive, breathes a deep breath
and sings like the senses of the world -
basso mountain chords, salt and sweet
palate of oceans and lakes, island
keys in major or minor, covered
by chromatic skies in grays and blues,
underscored in bird trill, while
rushing waters hide gold-scaled
fish swimming in smooth legato,
as deserts, cleft by forgotten storms,
notated by darker dunes, empty
arteries of sand, carry hooded riders
on horseback, rough-voiced, calling
to each other through heat and wind.

Hurricane

Kitty Jospe

I am Eve
             freshly expelled
from the garden, with a terrible fear
of worms, so bad some of my friends
will say it calls for a kalsarikännit—
that misattributed term for getting
drunk at home in your underwear—

I resemble my friend Eventual:
we both will need therapy for overcoming
anxiety disorders, especially since
worms will inevitably be part
of our final recycling.

You might wonder how this works
for a hurricane? Ask my third-cousin
twice-removed, Tea of Heaven,
with periwinkle petals
lined with varicose veins.
She will tell you to look me in the eye,
but to beware of my clutter and clatter
of horseshoes never requested— and cast
out iron words like actinomorphic.

I am not pleased to wreak havoc,
wreck all that has been built by man.
After all, there are a few noble testimonies
to the greatness of humanity.
And then there are the rest of you—
like poor limpets clinging to rocks,
hiding your tongues inside your shells,
waiting for the tide to recede.

The point is, I don't want to stay as
temporal com trovões when I go to Brazil,
or tordenvejr when I tear through the North Sea.
I just want to be a change in wind,

pass like evening.

Duplex thinking of all those fallen in war, fallen prey to accidents,
fallen prey to bad circumstances, fallen and unable to rise

Kitty Jospe

I begin with fall, as in autumn,
as in leaves floating down

as in how what leaves might float down
not up, as the seasons take turns

as in the the as in taking a turn
to try to explain falling

as in stumbling, falling
to your knees, by accident or prayer

as in on your knees, by accident, praying
this not be the end,

of so much: not the end
of our seasons, our earth, of a chance—

the chance to do right by another, instill kindness
no matter the season; I begin with fall.

Mother Nature Has Her Way

Mary Louise Kiernan

praying mantis kneels
break dawn   mosquitos quiver
coupling in mid-air

leaves cluster porchside
curled horseshoe crab shells on stems
matchless for wet wind

marble rain bombards
Gaia rages ice sparks fire
cracks her thunder whip

A Poetry Reading in Bushwick

Ron Kolm

A darkening sky gives warning
Hurrying me down
From the elevated subway platform
To the streets below.
A quiet neighborhood doesn't mean
That it's safe. A car slows
And the driver glares at me
Then accelerates and leaves
With a screech of tires.
Frightened, I duck into the building
Where the reading has already started.
The participants are very touchy feely
But they are also pretty good poets
So I exhale, and decide to stay.

Patricide

Susan Konz

You will not make me grovel
Slouch back through the muck
you come from
Your axe bent vigil
to the ghost of hemlock trees
rooted deep in tar black soil
Coal choked heart
stayed in this forest
but I am not weak
like you
My back is straight
My arrow shoots
to kill

To See Like James Clerk Maxwell*

Darcie Kortan

On the electromagnetic spectrum—
the range of waves across the universe
from radio waves to gamma rays—
the human eye can see but a rainbow sliver.

Imagine floating in the water.
You can see and feel waves rocking you close by, but
as waves shorten toward the beach, they disappear;
as waves lengthen out to sea, they disappear.
The world you see is but a small cove of choppy water,
the rest of the ocean eerily invisible.

Thoughts roil my mind from the moment I wake
till sleep eclipses my consciousness.
To-do lists and gripes and retorts I wish I'd spoken
flood my cerebrum with ghost messages
that yet make my existence glow,
flickering light through a tube of invisible neon,
a red OPEN sign that leaves my mind NO VACANCY.

And beyond the small cove
of my anxious existence
are waves of consciousness
imperceptible to me:

Over the horizon to my right,
the peak and frequency is fast—
a beach of calm where small breakers
curl my breath,
crash over and over.

Over the horizon to my left,
a briny deep devoid of ideas
spawns a wave trough wide enough
to lift and lower a container ship (my ego locked inside)—
mind's vast spectrum of peaks and valleys,
all without a single thought,
without a single word.

                              *discovered the electromagnetic spectrum, 1865

Jackie 1 1966   silver silk screen print, Andy Warhol

Raphael Kosek

after Allen Ginsberg and the Rolling Stones

America, America, you always
put your feet up on the table, entered
through the windows, embraced
Jacksonian rough edges, the brute
strength of a populous emboldened
by ignorance, guns and a flag,

but Jackie gave you Camelot—a royalty
all your own with Chanel suits,
a White House artfully restored
under her Frenchified eye—
Jackie's je ne sais quoi,
but you stomped it out, your boots
deconstructed her slender elegance,
the pillbox hat that rode so lightly,
always detesting her slightly
better-than-you demeanor,
yet prizing her European cachet.

America, you killed the Kennedys,
even when you cried pretty with
little John Junior at the funeral—
and you lamented again when
the god of death plucked his plane
out of the sky—so unfortunate.
You gave Jackie what for when she
married Onassis, and Warhol silvered
her smile forever to haunt you with hope,
to shame you—that pink suit, pathetic
and elegant after all, properly greyed,
darkened, blasphemed by the blood
you know will come.

Grandma's Honey Cake

Don Krieger

Dad repossessed a car from up north,
one of those Unsafe at Any Speed.
He couldn't manage it
on the two-lane

so I drove the whole way
Daytona to Rocky Mount.
I was fifteen
and loved every minute.

We dropped it at a bank in Philly,
rented a car and on to Newark.
Uncle Bill and Irma were in the kitchen,
Grandma and Rose upstairs

Rose had caught brain fever at thirteen.
She was still bright and kind, her face
gaunt and twisted, one arm and both legs

useless.

She stared at me, clutched my hand, kissed my face
loved what she saw
the bright promise she had lost

overnight.

Dad was delighted
with Grandma's honey cake.
He ate two pieces. I did too.

It was dry as dust.

On Valentine's Day, 2018, an intruder murdered 17 and injured 17 more at Stoneman Douglas High School in Parkland Florida. A year later, Sidney Aiello and a second unnamed Parkland survivor, and Jeremy Richman, the father of a child murdered in 2012 at Sandy Hook Elementary, all committed suicide in the same week.

Memorial Day, 2019

Don Krieger

Ninety miles upriver from Washington,
the flag at the Blue Goose Market
flew for a year at half-mast.

Was a child of Maryland
killed last year at Parkland?
And why was it

that since those survivors' suicides this March,
as I passed by on the highway,
roof open to the sun and spring air,

the flagpole was empty? But no,

none of that makes sense,
for though twenty of our warriors
killed themselves this month,

a new flag flew on Memorial Day
so huge that at half mast
it would touch the ground.

iPhone

Katherine Latella

I took such good care of you:
heeded mom's advice not to text from the toilet,
bought you a $40.00 case,
plugged you in so you could recharge,
wiped your face when you had a smudge.

I want you to know
the panic when your screen went black mid-call.
How I pressed the on button,
for ten seconds, twenty, a minute.
No life.

TAXI!
we sped to the Apple Store,
were told to wait
behind phones with minor illnesses:
cracked screens, poor battery –
MOVE US TO THE FRONT, I yearned to shout.
THIS IS LIFE OR DEATH!

Finally,
they ran tests.
I gazed at you, my darling,
stared into the camera,
wondered if you were
somewhere in there
beneath the plastic and the wires.

There's nothing that can be done.

You were so young.
Just a year and a half,
a toddler.

As they took you away from me,
for your parts,
I wondered if someday
there will be another phone
with your
circuit board,
microphone,
speaker,
battery,
heart.

On Days Like This   **Finalist**

Bonnie Law

On days like this
I forget that my voice matters,
that I am not standing on a precipice
screaming into the blackness,
which hears nothing.
That I mean something
to the people who love me
as I do them.

On days like this
I forget that the color of morning
and the mood of night,
are more than the culmination
of my losses.

Sphere

David Lawton

Carolina wagon wheel
Ruts road by haunted auction block
Spent trail of locomotive steam
Of where we been no more

Boll weevil drills a cotton flower
Chaw juice congealed in brass spittoon
Field hollers circle Rocky Mount
Through barefoot bluesman's sound

Manhattan brownstone rolling the bones
Neighborhood kids play at Ring-o-leavio
Barrelhouse keys turn rag player roll
Hopscotch girls do the chalk line stroll

Sister's teacher runs through scales
In room next door Monk's fingers trail
Round San Juan Hill the cats keep stride
'Cross gramophone the needle glides

Church organ renders gospel meet
Palms upward face towards heaven's seat
Hands laid upon flush demons out
Ecstatic spirit animates Ring Shout
                        'round about
                                  Cutting sesh
                                            Bop beret

Swivel chair   cigarette   cascades
Skull cap   blast cap   beads of sweat
Karakul   thread unspools   a spinner in a mill
Concentration   contemplation   an iridescent bloom

Foot pedals   flower petals   straw coolie hat
Crepuscule   Sufi whirl   hammered space between
In walked Bud   thick as blood   lost cabaret card
Talk back   blackjack   Ain't that a bitch?
                       Too ugly
Deepening sinkhole   sucking drain
            Then just walk away
          The music still turning in a groove
   A   mosaic   star   to   spin   on.

Daughters of Destiny

Rain Lee

A murderess.
A housewife.
A diagnosis.

What makes a woman a woman?

Big-breasted fire-brimming force of nature
Flag-toting revolutionist
Four foot three lolitas
Nasty woman
Ice queen
Straight-A Korean chick
Black Brooklyn girl, the world's your oyster.

We are not dolls, ornaments, cigar ashes to be ground under heels.

We are the daughters of baba-yagas and witches
Stuff of trailblazers, lawyers, activists, poets
Not mere Madonnas and thick-fleshed, lipsticked mannequins.

Forget not Kali the tightrope walker,
jewel-dipped and blazing,
Twirling madly round the moon.

Nor Helen Keller
Musician of touch and smell,
Sensuist and peacekeeper.

Forget not Nina Simone,
Her jazz anthems, tenacity, voice of civil rights
Nor Judy, helping lost ones search for their rainbow.

Let us release the genie from the bottle

And become

daughters of destiny.

Rivers and Gardens

Phillip X Levine

the strongest argument against war is the nature of war
the strongest argument against war is the nature of war

The river is Jordan
and the Garden's gone wild
a corruption of flowers
and the rupture of seed
the sky bleeds and blows
clouds and people to pieces
these are not pretty petals
with their sudden bloom in crowded places
these tulips have no sweet
these roses have no name
the wine has turned
the bread has mold
the birthplace of the 3
may now bury a million
and here is a boy who has lost his shoes
below the knees

The river is Tigris
and the Garden is vile
roses torn from stem
who wears these thorns?
who cut these palms?
who parted these sands?
who razed this mecca?
Eden boils
a failure of seed
the apple is cut and rots
roots are ripped
ivy tangles
here is a boy who has lost his shoes
below his knees
and a father with no sons

The river is Euphrates
and the Garden is vile
armed and fertile
with something new and cruel
the pin is pulled
and ready for seed

The soil is plowed open with pits
green bolts to red
what bounty?
what harvest?
war is a crop
for fattening a few
and feeding no one
rain cuts a man into parts
this piece was his leg, here lies his arm
these things used to belong to him
the bloom is off the rose
and in the powder
what tills this soil?
what waters these wounds?
here is a boy who has lost his shoes
below his knees
and a mother with no sons

the strongest argument against war is the nature of war

The river is Hudson
and the Garden's gone wild
Here is a boy who's lost his shoes
below his knees
And a father and mother with no sons
this is the season of bolt and ruin
and the bruising of fruit
here is the shrinking vine
the drift root and the idle rain
where is the spring sprout?
how is this harvest fall?

The river is Potomac
and the Garden is vile
Here, everywhere,
are boys who have lost their shoes
below their knees.

Friday the 13th*   **Finalist**

Heller Levinsom

WOR studios 1953   thelonious Monk/Sonny Rollins
sloop-de-sloop whirl wind full intake reed fill throat splash slippery slant
peek-a-boo inebriate   peregrinate   in-
cubate   square spiral boulder-roll stroll crab colossal   hi-hat crisp
chink snap crystalclarioncrystalline   bosomy broth ivories wrought
bath breadload beatitude
concuss allude   wedge hook link   sinkseepagelodge
                                                laurel sling
                                                carrion fletch

                     b e t r o t h
      clump stump flummery block lump here
         come de Monk   scruff scamper liv-
ery lurch   paint a birch   fu-
rl fistful conflagrate agitate French horn — fog-caster, frog-hopper —
conflate titillate aerate
levitate brindle lop Bird-bop

                                        chordal congregation?
                                        hymnal meditation
                        scintilla aubergine

whisk brisk bask peculiar challenge the ruler
adumbrate gestate
spray a mandate
, man

        * This poem hinges to the Monk tune "Friday the 13th."

Interlude in the Garage

Maria Lisella

Throw it all out, the photos, the papers, just toss it.
Your words to my ears but not my heart ... years
later I shuffle through bloated banker boxes piled,
re-arranged, but not gone -- fat with promises, curses,
copious notes, dreams, short stories, self-help clips.

So I waited, waited, waited for the right moment,
the right season, the right weather, right stage
of the moon, waited for the stars to be aligned with
your sun sign, your ascendant, waited for mercury
to emerge from its retrograde status that slows us

all down, keeps us from technology, from car accidents,
warns us to avoid anything new and for me, anything new
would be just this: clearing out a life, a writing life replete
with half-finished novellas, translations, layers of handwritten
anything, projects in midair, saturated with energy so palpable

it chases me out of the garage onto the street, into something
safer, away from the particles of the dead, from the random
places – under trees, around bookshelves, down in pits,
cartons of words, words, words, some in the light, others in
the dark, stumbling as I do over prickly discoveries, journals

so private that when you were breathing my eyes would
just glimpse stray words, but never invade an entry,
so I waited for the snow to fall, to be cleared, waited
for the humidity to run dry as a desert in New York, shifted
boxes, returned some books to your shelves in the apartment ...

dreading each time the door closed I'd be the last one out.

A Gift of Hammers...

Maria Lisella

After I inherited my father's car,
I found hammers all over the interior:
in a pocket on the door, under the
driver's seat, for sure in the trunk.

Had he planned to hammer his way
out of a drowned car, submerged into
a river, or if on one of his drives, he'd
imagined he'd let go of the wheel

fly off a bridge into a lake,
As an engineer, he tried to be prepared
for all of it: lightning, twisters, hurricanes
or were the hammers a form of self-defense?

Once he was nearly kidnapped by a small gang
of people who had been waiting outside doctors'
offices where old people would come out dazed
or distracted and they would offer to escort them

to their cars but would wallop them and slip them
into the gangs' cars, call their families, demand ransom.
We laughed at the scheme as the criminals were
in the wrong neighborhood for collecting any kind

of bounty worth the trouble of getting a senior
who might be incontinent, or about to have
a heart attack into their cars in the first place.

So I understood the self-defense hammers
Since I was an adolescent, he'd tried to teach me
and my sisters basic self-defense moves
and we'd follow the moves like running a comb

under an attacker's nose, walking with splayed keys
in hand, we'd memorize the choreography
thinking that running faster might be the best option
Once he equipped us with spray cans of mace

to blind attackers but who would want to be
that close to actually use it? One dainty hammer
had a bird like head atop a slim handle made
for a woman's hand another was robust, masculine

and heavy, its handle worn and smooth,
the striations of hickory or ash, beech
or boxwood, all stronger with age, a fact not
lost on my father and his choice of tools.

Noise
       -for Samantha-

Brian Liston

Noise,
Scream, whisper
Amplifies, numbs, stresses
World until we ask for, crave

Silence

Red-eyed on the Red-eye

Timothy Liu

Time off for grief
stuns me. I won't
go into it with
strangers seated
at a boarding gate
waiting for the plane
to be taken back
to a service hangar
due to mechanical
failure—another
plane given
a 50-50 chance
of helping me
get to the funeral
on time. I am one
you might call
pushy, demanding
an agent to find
an empty seat
on another flight
without wanting
to tell everyone
what my story is—
bereavement
something I don't
want to indulge in
too much if you
know what I mean?
Have you ever felt
cold but not cold
enough to ask
someone to throw
a blanket over you?
just give me one

of every drink
on that cart coming
down the aisle—
bladder full as you
crawl over others
to get some relief
only to discover
the way is blocked?
Seems unseemly
sobbing to myself
in a window seat
and being asked
by an attendant
if there's anything
else I need—half
of a crowded plane
already fast
asleep in coach—
legs cramped,
triple feature
on a seat back
pushed right up
to my face—nose
grease on a touch
screen where I
watch amid
real turbulence
two fighter pilots
on a blockbuster
summer sequel
having it all out—

Bela and the Rats

Julie Lomoe

Ages ago, in 1966, I abandoned my first marriage
And moved downtown to a rat-infested loft
In lower Manhattan, on Broome Street.
Rent was cheap. The ruthless developer Robert Moses
Wanted to ram an expressway through the heart
Of the historic cast iron district later known as SoHo.
Living in lofts was still illegal, but I took the risk,
My sole companion a gray Persian cat named Bela
I'd adopted when still an undergrad at Barnard,
Named for Bartok, not Lugosi.

Weaving back home from some forgotten party,
Drunkenly trudging up the endless stairs,
Unlocking the steel gray bars of my Fox lock,
I staggered in semi-darkness to my bed,
Sank onto the mattress. Hitting the pillow,
My cheek encountered something warm and hairy.
Shrieking, I jumped out of bed, yanked the chain
Hanging from the bare bulb overhead.
A giant rat lay slaughtered on my pillow,
Its throat ripped open by my devoted cat. A halo of blood
Around the head and neck, but nothing eaten,
Everything intact—Bela's offering to his mistress.

I knew my share of rats back in those years
Later labelled the Swinging Sixties.
These rats were men. The Pill was new,
AIDS an undiscovered virus
Lurking in apes in African jungles.
Powered by pot and rock and roll,
Sex was easy and casual. No promises,
No commitments. By and large,
The coupling was consensual.
Beneath their hippie long-haired looks,
Most men were gentlemen, not rats.

We talked before we fucked.
None shocked me with a kiss
The instant we met,
None grabbed my pussy.
The rats were a minority.

Still, there were encounters
We'd now condemn as date rape,
Like the man who made
Stretchers for my paintings,
Who refused rejection. It took all my strength
To wrestle him down the battleship gray stairs
Of my Broome Street loft. One shove
Could have cracked his skull, but I refrained.
Soon he became a famous artist.

Googling the Broome Street Expressway,
I found a listing for a loft at 456 Broome,
My old address. They want
Three and a half million.
SoHo has cachet—
Heath Ledger overdosed and died
In a loft across the street.

I can't afford the cost of SoHo any more,
Can't afford the cost of casual promiscuity.
Those days are decades in the past.
I don't regret them, but if time travel were an option,
I'd say fuggedabout it. Give me the here and now.
Still, when I hear the vitriolic rants of misogynistic pigs
Who want to ban abortion,
I realize progress is a delusion.
The rats have multiplied.
Women, high time to unsheathe our claws.

Core Value

Phil Lynch

Pare back to the core and then more,
remove the silk and satin layers
reveal the bare within
feel the dips
and curves
the texture of the velvet
and the rough, observe each blemish,
talk about the odd bits, the shapes that do not fit,
spare no blush, disabuse yourself of the notion of perfection,
rejoice in all you have laid out and learned. Here you will find
where to begin.

A Voice in The Produce Aisle

Betty MacDonald

A voice in the produce aisle,
"Ms. McCarthy!"A
That's not my name,
but I know he means me.

I turn to see a friend I've known for twenty years,
I hardly ever see him,
Our contact has been unique.

We sat next to each other
at two different country weddings
over many years.
The bride the same on both occasions,
marrying a different man each time.

The first time a youthful fling
Likely ended
with the formality of the wedding.

The second time
The couple's vows to love till death
seemed to be working,
so far at least.

I pause next to the avocados as we catch up.
He inquires about a mutual friend.
"She no longer speaks to me." I respond.

"I don't really like her," he admits.
"I still like her," I counter,
"But we're no longer friends."

Drive — Finalist

Mary Makofske

birth's hard journey   then the smooth ride home
safety belt   air bag   child-proof lock
traveling concert   moveable feast   (Are we there yet?)
squabbles in the back seat   He punched me!   I did not!

beware the careless door that loves to catch
boy's thumb   dog's tail   prom dress   wedding gown
driving under the influence   of drink   of drugs   of youth
drive-in bank   drive-in movie   drive-in restaurant
waitress on skates bearing tray through the parking lot

drive-by shootings   drive-by viewings at drive-by cemeteries
bootleg liquor in the rumble seat   bomb under the chassis
truck left on the frozen lake   bets on when it will sink
kids belted in under water   weeping mother
describing the carjacker she made up

Aztek   Cherokee   Cheyenne   Comanche   Dakota   Navaho
Explorer everyone wants to be   (Are we there yet?)
road rage   road trip   road movie   drag race
Nascar drivers going nowhere fast
brake   brake   accelerator   brake   give 'er the gas

parallel parking   back parking   double parking
parking   what a concept   boudoir on wheels
how many conceptions occurred in back seats?
drive till the wide-eyed baby sleeps

Volkswagen bug   Corvette   Model T   Lincoln touring car
the bloody President and his wife with her splattered pink suit
driving over the line   the squirrel   the skunk   the snake
the cat   the dog   the child   the cliff   (Are we there yet?)

getaway car   car that can't get away
in clotted arteries on the way to work
Princess Di barreling into the tunnel
car lunging off Chappaquiddick Bridge

gun rack   spare tire   jack up the car   (Are we there yet?)
cruising for smack   cruising for girls   driving while black
license and registration   get out of the car
spread your legs   put your hands on the hood

limousine gliding by with its darkened windows

first scratch   breakdown   crash
pack in the luggage   the contraband   the body
tail fins   tail spins   failed inspection   running on empty
the plush bed in the hearse

The Door Rattles When She Steps In

John Martucci

The door rattles when she steps in.
The floors creak in agreement.
The birds wait their turn to twitter.
And trees sway in the wind

The windows rattle when she calls.
The clouds reply with thunder's voice,
hail hammers the rain gutters
and traffic slows to a crawl.

Foundations falter when she finds fault.
The walls, like curtains, tremble.
The furniture vibrates, slides askew,
And knickknacks fall from the shelves.

The breeze whistles when she sings
The sun shines down on every note
The birds return in harmony
And thunder stops to listen

Public Safety Announcement

Prince McNally

1) This is for the women,
   who ignore the red flags.

2) This is for the women,
   who refuse to leave.

3) This is for the women,
   who leave and return.

4) This is for the women,
   who believe he will change.

5) This is for the women,
   who think they'll change him.

6) This is for the women,
   who see a whole other side to him.

7) This is for the women,
   who make excuses for him.`

8) This is for the women,
   who believe he truly loves them.

9) This is for the women, who believe him
   when he says he won't hurt them again.

10) This is a **Public Safety Announcement for Domestic Violence:**
The next time he hits you, and he will hit you again, he just might—kill you.

The Shift Forman's Daughter

Tana Miller

daddy came marching home from
the second World War
hopeful   wanting more
the army had tested him
deemed him highly intelligent
trusted him to install radar
he had glimpsed
the world beyond Alabama
wasn't about to follow

his silent father and shovel clinker
in faded work clothes   waste his life
eating dust in a stinking hot cement plant

he followed every lead every hint
dressed every morning in a starched white shirt
it was not enough
jobs were scarce with all the men
pouring home after the war
he wasn't qualified for much
he stopped trying   talking   laughing

he ignored his pretty teen-aged wife
who was damn tired of living with her
wild-eyed Bible quoting mother-in-law
he never held me   a stranger born while
he was at war in the South Pacific
a daughter he didn't know enough to love
stuck in his parents' spare room
by the railroad tracks   he drank whiskey at night
told his wife the train's whistle broke his heart

mama got pregnant again
daddy hated her womb
for sucking in his sperm
preparing to spit out one more
fussy mewing child
to feed shelter
he had night terrors
woke up the whole family   sweating
screaming crying   night-after-night

he watched his silent father
put on his khaki work clothes
go to work at the plant
come home   eat cornbread crumbled
in a tall glass of buttermilk
wash his feet   go off to bed
one Monday daddy came home
said he'd been offered a shift foreman's
job at a cement plant in Fairborn, Ohio

pack up he told mama
and went to bed
before he had any supper

Halloween Leafage

Ermira Mitre

The bird's chirping has gone silent tonight,
in its absence this fall tastes sour,
vacationers have emptied the beaches,
birds in V-shape have taken their flight,
leaving behind pristine images.
Leaves start migrating from trees,
while fall kicks off with sad feelings,
as moon tears through clouds
damping the darkness of the evening.

As transient vacationers on Earth,
the untethered souls wander
over fallen Halloween leafage
quivering like withered, fiery leaves,
waving their farewell wings,
to feel the earth, the wind, the flight.
then resting on a rock somewhere,
carving plenty implicit memories behind.

Memorabilia

Beth SK Morris

My mother was a thrower.
We moved too many times
in mother's attempt to better
herself and each time
we changed our address
or she had a fight
with a family member
she purged more and more
of our history.

She gave our oldest son
my father's watch and gold chain
for graduation. He claimed
they were stolen after he left home
for Florida but I suspect he sold
them for food or rent money.
I gave my youngest son
my father's jade ring.
Haven't seen it in twenty years.

I rescued the "Modern Library"
collection, our ration cards
from WWII, copies of the books
my father wrote. My nephew took
the photo album and the chess set.
But I have letters replete
with Polonius-like advice and
my father's pencil-scrawled,
yellowed notebook.

to that child hiding in the bomb shelter

K.R. Morrison

    i'm coming –

    soon i'll scoop you up   with you feel earth
    mother kick down war & border doors

    for us, sea crones wash away
    their grenades while I strap you to me
    with poet's dynamite

to that child hiding in the bomb shelter

    i'm coming –

    i hear   your love cries   your tears
    i gasp   for you   i hold my breath

    in dreams   your cherry innocence sings
    to me   child ghosts echo   in zephyr winds

to that child hiding in the bomb shelter

    create tents from flags stitched in freedom
    tell your mother a magic story

    into the wall draw a space portal
    into it   shove fear
    their genocides   their tanks

Tell your friends to stuff prayers in their pockets
with me, i'm bringing the sun.

We got a whole crew
taking to the streets, for you.

Rainbow, A Week After Going to the Photoville Festival 2023 Brooklyn Bridge Park, NY — Finalist

Karen Neuberg

This rainbow
    does not erase

what I, not wanting
    still see

without still seeing ...
    container 26, video

Mariupol, Ukraine
    bodies being rolled

mass grave
    shovelfuls of dirt.

I know enough
    to know, right now,

there is keening somewhere
    both human and more than human

while before me,
    this rainbow these children laughing.

Like a hand reaching out
>   ~ after Michelangelo's "Hand of God: The Creation of Adam"

Mary Newell

not down from highest heaven -
>   g-d knows, we tire of hierarchy

nor like Michelangelo's hoary white guy,
>   creating through cosmic fiat
>>   aided by cherub hoard transporting him through florid space,
>>>   his arm around a pretty young thing

and Adam looking quite alive already,
>   pumped, though languid
>   ready to take his role, commanding
>>   that whole green-brown creation -
>>>   surely his show of maleness grants the right

>   More like hands uplifting,
>>   an Atlas, bearing a spinning orb -
>>>   a force of anti-gravity
>>>   to keep us vertical,

>>   aspiring

>>   despite the heaviness
>>   of time

but unburdened, freed of striving
>   a hand that beckons through a wind-sprung portal

>>   proffering

Seventy and Counting
> Our lives are defined by opportunities; even the ones we miss
> —Benjamin Button

Perry S. Nicholas

Maybe like Benjamin Button I will age
backward, a being growing younger as he
moves ahead in his life, inch by inch.

I walk toward a mother's voice calling me
home for dinner after riding a bike,
father's bark when I pushed him too far.

In this fog, I wander, following
their ghostly voices in the night,
knowing in my right mind they are gone.

In my left, wishing for one more miracle,
but miracles happen only to mortals
who don't play by the rules, discern too much,

believe in both taken and missed opportunities.
Maybe like Benjamin I will age, as I crawl closer
to the beginning, stop gracefully when I reach the start.

Dear Han Shan

Will Nixon

I'm afraid Starbucks no longer serves Samurai Tea,
but don't you dare come down from your hermit's cave.
I need your foolishness teaching ravens to curse in karaoke
& chipmunks to quit chattering manifestos of impotent rage.
Sure, we have the American gopher for cheap entertainment
& geckos grown wealthy on TV, but nothing can match
your wine-barrel belly laugh, your begging bowl left out
in the rain. You've married & divorced ten thousand trees.
You're the crazy uncle who brings lightning to weddings &
somehow hoodwinked our mayor out of our favorite parade.
Your philosophy has fermented in a cave where spiders
never complain. Han Shan, your rags smell like bear shit,
but your breath is a fern. Your black-nailed toes--a crime
against walking. Yet we still read your poems carved into
beech bark or tucked under moss where only salamanders
may squirm. They say nobody can teach Shakespeare to a tree,
& they're right, but you've persuaded stars to spill light on
thousands of nights & hemlocks to hold tight caked in ice.
Han Shan, I'm afraid Starbucks no longer sells Samurai Tea,
but they do sell CDs of Chinese philosophers laughing
like boulders tumbling down mountainsides after reading
your poems. May you never come down from your joy.

Lucy

John O'Conner

Probably around 3 in the morning
she had begun to dose. Yes, you're
correct to point out they didn't count
time in that manner.
They would say it was night,
if they had words, and that the growling
below her had subsided. So when her grip
loosened she fell. And fell.
Do you know anyone who has fallen
so long? And yet they found her.
And now they know from whence she fell.

I've done a different kind of falling
through the centuries. And it never
fails that someone will pick me up
and help me back into the tree
before the hyenas get too close,
the savanna expanding quietly
below a grueling sun. The last time
I fell it was next to someone
who had shattered everything,
leaving behind a secret hidden
in her crazy bone. You think
you know me?, she said.

At Coney Island, she came on after
the swordswallower. A foot
where the shoulder should be.
Her jawbone held in her hand,
ready to do battle. Walk along
the Boardwalk after the show
and listen to the pumping sea
asking the same question it has asked
everyone for a billion years.
Where does your salt come from?
When are you going to give it back?

Gnomen

(an object, such as the style of a sundial,
that projects a shadow used as an indicator)

Irene O'Garden

For all that Earth is solid,
mineraled and flush,
her density is shadow
to emotion's blazing push

from center outward. Every
being's feelings leaping, flaring
everynow: our crackling globe
of longing, flailing, scarring,

larking, thrilling and relief
arcs in dazzling twists   --
a massive sizzling electric sphere
invisible to old mad scientists.

But thanks to them our Earth
is mirroring those motions—
tremors, traumas,
arcing ash and oceans.

An omen tells a future,
but a gnomon tells
the moment, holding light
and shadow on a dial.

Finite, finite planet—
yet infinite our feelings—
lasering those vivid rays
occasions, in the moment, healing.

Again & Again, the Berkshires

Michael O'Mara

Woven roadside bushel baskets brimming with delicious reds. Our old man splurging, like he did midsummer, for one of sweet ears we'd shuck outdoors, boil in a thirty-quart stock pot that came with the tiny house outfitted like a bunkbed hunter's shack. The kitchen, a single-file obstacle course of catalog cabinets with built-in sink, three-burner enameled electric range, & a ten-cube slouch- shouldered icebox, generally more frost & ice than box, with a latch lock that said this may be the most important door in the house. It did hold the old man's beer.

Were we happy? I don't think that was even a question then. We didn't church on Sundays to learn about happiness.

Our friends lived among the farms but none were farmers. One's dad made ball-point pens. One had no dad at all, just an auntie. Another's made Hueys for the war. Ours made holes in the ground for work & for weekend fun.

It may have looked good in a sweater & scarf of autumn colors to the scent of neighbors burning leaves, or beneath the folded blue-white sparkling shrouds of winter snow fragrant with hard-wood hand-chopped & split & coaxed to flaming embers, but mostly our homestead looked like an open wound, like the bombed-out scapes of the old man's service in World War II to the chagrin of our enduring neighbors.

Eventually, even the river complained.

Dammed on either end, she lapped our shores, but with the spring thaw resurrected the old range our old man, too cheap to pay the dump fee, had interred in a poor man's promontory at the water's edge. Legs skyward in hopeless indiscrete rigor; it looked like the underside of a drowned bloated Holstein abandoned to the great flood.

I half-hobbled the front left leg, bending it to a 90 with one stroke of the 20-pound sledge that the old man wordlessly handed me & continued as I'd been taught: rest the hammerhead on the target, adjust a wide firm stance, lift into a backswing & let physics & the steel's weight do the work.

Once it showed weakness, exploit it. With that, each leg crumbled & then the bottom pan, the enameled sides.

If I could have seen myself, I would have seen a boy shining, alternatively grimacing & smiling, tirelessly swinging & vibrating like a cartoon with the impact of each blow & just like a man, wouldn't I have been thinking that's not coming back & the very next spring —well, you know.

Even now in dotage dreams, side-eyed Holsteins graze,

dented & lame, among the high green soft grass.

Late Fall Sunset

Mary K O'Melveny

The guardian of the sky teases me
with stripes of amber, pale rose,
crimson, peach blossom. Shadows
of mauve, blue mix it up with pale
white clouds, streaked with ivory
lace. A hint of grey shadow, floats
back forth like a silent dance partner.
Beneath this flagrant color field, fall
foliage pales, retreats from memory.
Sky is all we see, All we wish to know.

The clock has shifted back one hour.
As chilled air settles across open fields,
I reach for sweater, jacket, wool scarf.
Such a sunset is a natural trickster.
I can believe that winter is still far
away, that all those missing birds who
once pinwheeled overhead can be replaced
by swirls, splashes of colored lights.
The guardian of the sky teases me
that I can sprout wings, be airborne.

October

Kathy Poppino

Bird house with a slat missing
till attracts the titmice, chickadees
grand cardinal and his mate,
the house twirling on a string
as they spar for seed.
The chickadee's uneven flying path
scoops down, rises up small
and down again as he heads for the goal.
The cardinal rules – no other birds
can stay while he feasts, the titmice
fall away, diving over the side.

Leaves and pine needles litter everything.
Bittersweet has popped its reds in a vast nest above
the yews like a glorious crown.
Nobody can pass on the path below
because the stately weight
bends forward the massive green branches.

...despite the omission from the contents page
I am documented in every cell of ontological being

Siobhan Potter

You did not come into this world naked. You arrived clothed in want—
to be recognised by the wound that will kill you. The inhabitants of this world
will not receive you in any other way. Perhaps, one planet further from, you will learn to die
unfettered by hope's disabling crutch. And those left behind, will long for
the tall quiet woman mistaken as the groundskeeper and the garden there is no going back to where
Hiberna dreamed up cherries...

Sight

Linette Rabsatt

I faded
like primary colors fade
when they are mixed with white
like the moon disappears
when the sun shines bright
not unlike my heart
when my mood is not right
I've got stains on my hand
because food security is the fight
complex and crazy
to sore eyes, I'm the sight
the key is a puzzle
to take you into the light
it has all the right colors
to get you ready for the flight
looking for your ticket?
it's turquoise, yellow, and green
with pink highlights
neatly packaged and
all enveloped in white

November 2020 (a Thanksgiving pantoum)
    inspired by Joy Harjo's "Perhaps the world ends here"

Carrie Magness Radner

When bones are no longer alive,
flesh is cut away, cleaned by sharp teeth
as hungry humans and animals gather to give thanks.
Even when loved ones meet up virtually

flesh is cut away, cleaned by sharp teeth.
Zooming hot with bellies and hearts full—
Even when loved ones meet virtually,
the world begins at the dining table.

Zooming hot with bellies and hearts full;
when other babies are born, and secrets and news are shared,
the world begins at the dining table.
We will remember our loved ones gone

when other babies are born, and secrets and news are shared
as hungry humans and animals gather to give thanks.
We will remember our loved ones gone
when our bones are no longer alive.

ordinarily, she marched
    — Uvalde

Suzanne S. Rancourt

along trails popcorned with variant sized pebbles
stones imposed pressure up through
mixed hardwood forest floor

right angled shoulders, head, hips, sigmoid spine
slithers emergent expressions into a tripping
stumbling gait, sends even keen hikers

seeking purchase, acute longing for rebalance
correct and return to a level path without incidents
proper placement among things

that matter when crisp wind rattles classic leaves
autumnal in their cliches and overuse ordinarily
nothing would be said about the false dropping

flesh encounters with age while falling sounds
we walk among, kicking through leaf piles once
raked by hand and lower abs now blown noisily

but here on this trail where north grown moss consumes
old pine stumps with sweet decomp scent, the rot enthralls
starry spirals 'cross the white pine needles ground covering

camouflaged chipmunk-tunnel-holes these striped torpedoes
propel for expulsion up through silo tree trunks
explode among squirrel and blue jays' racket

protest existence, rapid loss, clear cutting, skidders
exodus, ground pounding timber umpff
with a bounce slo-mo recoil displacement

and no one is safe from this progress that rides
on round files and chainsaw sharpening jigs
we are all consumers, we are all feeding

ordinarily, she marched but today is for staggering
under the waiting, the confirmation, from ouroborol All Stars,
green canvas sneakers – all sold out

gift of moon she clenched with teeth

Suzanne S. Rancourt

she does not hold the moon in her hands.
she flies through grievous air
a pearl sabot with razor edge cleaves
more than slices more than tears
more than some simple easement a seamstress picks & rips -
laser hot fleshing edge - cut darkness from an ignorant shroud
her teeth threaten to crumble, jaws tremble
for this moon is a thrown discus
not a boomerang
not a javelin, atlatl lightning bolt
it is milk white on the verge, just this side
of scalding rage changing forever
the proteins' thickening skin - one must scry
with index finger - swirl counter in this cosmic kettle
peel this hairless flesh from steaming liquid

she does not hold the moon in her hands
burnt from whiteness - scarred - below boiling point
and pulls copper bottomed saucepans off flames
flings open the front door
hammer-throws lightning bolts back into sky
clenched between her teeth a ligament white moon
the shape of a dog smile
there is no need to remain at the burner
when an arrow to the sky is the same
as a moon disc filleting the universe

Feathers

Guy Reed

Sitting on the living room floor
absorbing the call. A poet
jumped from a bridge.
Just two weeks ago,
sitting next to him—
so encouraging, eager
for poetry, art, ideas. Now
I cannot speak to him—
right next to each other
in a gallery, metal folding chairs,
his face turned to mine, inches away
and now he knows what death is
if the dead have knowledge of it.

A small white feather floats down
and lands in my lap. John Lennon
told his son Sean that if there's life
after death, as a sign, he'd float a white feather
across the room. This feather, loose
from a pillow or a down coat, blown
into the air by a forced-air furnace.

Once before, sitting in the yard
grieved by a relative's passing
a single white feather drifted out of
the clear sky and landed at my feet.
Naturally occurring and so well timed.
Birds shed feathers. Gravity, mass,
and air flow, trajectory meets a still point.

A spirit must weigh less than a dust mote
having to fall somewhere after being let go.

I've seen feathers out in the world,
floating behind people in line at the bank,
drifting the grocery store aisle, sailing
the streets of the village, and there is
a rational explanation for each one, but then
we don't really know. What if the dead
are trying to get our attention? A feather
now the only thing they can move,
something that glories in its flight.

Warp and Weft

Liz Reilly

Riot and groan in the heat,
Love, love the brassy impulse
To break the motherskin,
To stretch wet in the humid dark,
Allowing the warp and weft of recollection
To part, and to let your body speak again.

There is nothing without this.

Take what you will, but there is nothing without
This scraping reach, this godless ecstasy.

Rise and fall, feast and fast,
Swallow the cool and calling waters
If that is what you want.

If that is what you want,
Part your tender lips on the sea,
Make romance of sacrifice,
And praise the empty gestures
Of blueboned deprivation.

Starve if you want to, but do not forget
There is nothing
Without your wild flame,
Crowding out from its calyx
To burn a passing prayer
On the walls of eternity.

Part the warp and weft of recollection,
Of fear and artifice,
And let your body bloom again.

Strikes

Donna Reis

My father loved to savor a rainstorm.
I'd join him under the corrugate, green
fiberglass held up by iron, scrolled posts.
We'd sit in those circular, straw chairs
that are now all the rage. I'd shriek
as lightening pierced the sky, and thunder
crashed and rumbled. Dad would say,
There he is. That's Rip Van Winkle
bowling. We'd listen. That's a strike.
I'd breathe in the metallic air cheering
Rip's perfect score knowing the stormy
evening with my father was perfect as well.

White Crosses

Sally Rhoades

bear the soldiers shot down,
blown up. Their screams
in death sudden as the carp
Breaks the water's skin.

Their voices silenced in youth,
their hometown suffers the loss
of one of their sons who won't
be coming home to take up

the plough, to be the grocer,
to sit in the village square and
talk with old men who had seen
war like theirs, felt the bombings
in their sleep, knew what Dying

was and how death made no
exception, whether you were
the butcher's son or the son
of the farm who milked the

cows in early morning's light.
There was no compensation
for death. It lived on the skin,
so mottled and trespassed.

These boys that lie under
those white crosses won't
be coming home to their
mother's smile or their

father's shoulder, who will
grieve an endless hole
created in their heart for
the unborn children, for

the half-lived life, for the
sounds of their laughter
in kitchen light. The
white crosses bear the

weight of battle and loss
that transcends horror.
That leaves a stone in
the heart of a grateful

Nation, no longer in the dark
with their freedom gone.
We weep for our dead, too
soon gone and bow our heads.

Black Moth

Cheryl A. Rice

When he dies, my first reaction is relief.
A month of horrible mystery ended
with his breath.
Then I think,
'everything is ruined,'
but I don't mean what is,
whatever has been,
but the potential, the dream
of what a family is
in movies, what a
brother and sister act like in sit-coms.

I see our sister and ask what I can do.
"I want my brother back!"
she cries, she who comforted him,
prepared his failing brain,
wiped sweat from his still forehead
while he died.
She asks for the one wish I cannot grant.

Then I decide I want to die, too,
not be left behind in this dark confusion,
brutality that surely cannot ease,
life that will never recover
just as he will never recover,
doctors only pinpointing a diagnosis,
your fatal illness
days before.

I believe only in blackness after death,
no pearly barriers,
angelic escorts, reunions with
all our previous dead.
I believe in energy release when the body fails.
I have as much of him as I ever had.

Black moth, crisp wings
beating on my screen door,
is as close to a sign as I dare,
white too hopeful a color for things beyond.
I could die, if I choose,
and maybe I will.
I have not yet committed to
any contract as such.
I will give it some time, see if
delight in anything returns.

Our sister sees signs,
needs them to believe there's something left here.
You and I, Brother, had an understanding of sorts,
mutual acknowledgement that maybe,
as two black moths ourselves,
the breeze our wings beat across the continent
continues as it will.

An Interruption

Stephen Roberts

I started writing poetry to share
my tragic life and the bitter
lessons I had learned
during my teenage years.
My ambition was to be
the voice of my generation,
chronicling the adolescent themes
of sexual longing
and suicidal ideation.
But this attracted the scrutiny of
stern adults instead of
cute girls so I stopped
writing poetry for a while
and started collecting books,
as if owning someone else's art
could be a substitute for mine.

Sweet

Heather Christy Robinson

This weekend my son told me
he straight-up doesn't like honey
and
my daughter told me she doesn't like boys
or rather, that she likes both boys and girls
or, head down eyes up, maybe just girls.
I don't understand
because we've always
had honey in our home,
so he was raised with it
just like I had been.
Of course, he also had Nutella
as an option, which I didn't
and maybe that is the difference.
What's weird for me
is that I want
to share the desire
for honey. I'm fine with Nutella.
It is dark and creamy
and can make one's mouth water,
but honey
comforts and soothes
and fills in all the spaces
in toasted bread,
and it's what I'm used to.

In Your Sleep

Tom Romeo

Sometimes when I wake up in the middle of the night
I stare at you.
I hope that doesn't sound too creepy.

You see, you smile in your sleep –
a beautiful, peaceful smile –
and I just can't look away.

Sometimes, you wake up
and catch me staring.
Then your smile widens to a grin

and in a slumber-sweetened whisper you say,
"You're loving me, aren't you?"
Yes. Yes, I am.

Shelling the Peas
for my grandmother

Amanda Russell

Big Momma's basket was always fuller than mine.
A pile of purple eyes, staring hard

as she split and slipped each pea
from the hull with nothing but muscle memory.

In the shade of the old oak tree, her short, raven hair
gleamed, marking the point where we all checked in.

From a distant branch on the magnolia tree,
I watched the afternoon sway its sweltering grace.

Visitors came and went like gusts of wind.
Laughter sprang up like color-popped bluebonnets.

Down the hill, the metal barn leaned into the forest
and whispered its rusted wreath of creaks.

The front porch of the house
was still a dream, and the deep freeze was full

of popsicles. Summer beaded us all a crown
of sweat, whether or not we earned it.

single-room oratorio, summer

Stephanie JT Russell

> Oh, abandonado!
> —Pablo Neruda, Song of Despair

The first or second morning,
you rocked me on a sleeping mat,
cow-dust-thin ticking drenched
in a thousand daybreak yawns.
Counterpoint to the pigeons' coo,
you sang an antique xota, mourning
a sailor who planted a field,
roses seeded with algebraic care,
only to leave before it bloomed.
The wanderlust I chose was you—
rebus chaparral, sole radius of agreement
a covenant of untamable change.

May's a good month to lay tap roots,
eighty square feet furnished end to end
with risk, a single easterly pane bursting
with promise of flight. Feasts for many
on a two-burner camp stove set out
on prayer rugs, ingots of edible liturgy.
Tiny kernels of light webbed out on wire,
glinting between us and cafe clatter below.

Black paper rolled on the roof in June
tarred every meter of soul, every half-moon
finger bed. My knees weren't bad then, but
going fast. I could still pattern cobblestones
in the dark, flat sides up, while I worked
head-down, ringed in by clinking ice and stale
barista coffee. Those crooked tables tipping
uneven against the lot were our eden of
apperception, tucked back from the curb in
smallest pretense of sanctuary.

Who was that donning my skin, morning
after the furthest fatality, canting on the sill
like a leaf-tailed gecko, mandible turned
to the sun? Fracaso final, the singer's whisper
predicted, and I chose to believe she was not
singing of us.

I'd gladly slip back in a minute to us twining
on the rooftop, copper church spire looming
above our sacramental calamity. Or better, the
moment at 4th and A when you came to me,
arms flung wide, smiling, cherry's petal
constellation scribing your rawboned arms.
Blooms fall like fading snow, as they always
ever will.

Done In

Stephanie JT Russell

Nothing much bigger than my fist survives
very long in the astringent earth beneath

the cedars we planted to buffer noise
and partition the grim summer heat.

Defying their nursery labels

    —long-blooming. acid-loving. drought resistant.—

and incongruent alkalinities suggested by my neighbor

    —eggshells. dolomite dust. mats clawed from
    the hairbrush.—

the flowers die, or adopt pretense of dying,
holding unembarrassed court in their ridged, ropy hides.

Their dessications make it hard to unhear the swish
of extinction's burning gown. And from there, wondering

how to dwell here if my husband is first to go. Will I end up
done in by uncoupled lethargy, conversing only with

snapdragons too lazy to fight for their own lives? I try
to make up the difference for them, for us, but it's useless:

no potion or silence can cool the weight of next year's
sunlight or this year's uncertain bloom.

Desired, or Not

Margaret R. Sáraco

an innocent red kiss impressed
on paper with a birthday pencil, a gift
to a happy student

the quick and meaningful kiss
to your child both with pursed lips
whimsical and loving

the unwanted kiss
a quick turn of the head
then uncomfortable peck on the cheek,

the woman at cliff's edge
in Klimt's Kiss, imbalanced,
the artist uses her beauty

to exert his prowess,
her head turns, ashamed
he, triumphant as we gaze

at her loveliness,
mesmerized by
the yellow and gold

and miss the rest.

Winterscape

Judith Saunders

Summer's grace is generous
and lush, winter's spare and chiseled,
its images indelible:
these ornamental grasses,
slender stems and tasseled tops
burnished and backlit
by low-angled sun,
platinum and yellow gold
against the glitter-glaze of snow
and piercing blue of sky
wrung dry by clarifying cold.

For My Father: The Cartographer

Jan Schmidt

I wish in the darkness of memory like
the buzz in the air on a windless snowy night
that the static was a clue
that the world inside you was real.
For your wasting time was not mine.

Your glazed eyes were hardly open.
You stared at specks
in the air   reached for them
as if your body had turned to dust
and you were gathering yourself in.

I wish now in your last days
there had been whispered nothings
instead of my unvoiced anger and dismay.

A long time ago in winter
on clear nights you traced patterns in the sky
flickering stars Orion The Little Dipper
The Big Dipper the North Star. Sometimes
you pointed out Venus burning white
bright unmistakably there after sunset.

And in summer you named the clouds.
Cirrus for calm clear days   cumulus
fluff balls heavy with water with wind
stratus for times of gray mist and fog
nimbus when the earth would rinse with rain.
The gods were weeping you said.

You mapped a universe for me.
I wish I could have shown you
the constellations of my love.

One Among Many

Moe Seager

I am first born
Son of my mother
Who married my father
And bore nine children
Buried our dead
Plain pine boxes
Thinly sewn into pockets of dirt
Mourning our kin
Kin of our neighbor

We give of our muscle
Our tenuous time
Pride in our part
Played in the world
We work to live, Live to love, Love to be
We walk this Earth together.

I toil day after day
and nights
A simple laborer
Simply making it.
One among many

On tired knees and weakly legs
What burdens my back can't carry
Weights my shoulders cannot withstand
What gifts too rich and plenty
For my small hands to hold
I share and share alike
One among many

Dream and dare
Embrace the world
Colors and tongues
Shape our lives
Room for All round table

High times, low times
Sometimes all we have
Courage and trust
The bond between us
Between times
We do the best we can
For troubled waters
Rush and they swirl
Rushing and swirling
About us all
Upstream we surge
Surging and spawning
Spilling ourselves
One among many

I march, I run
I sit and calm
Oh let go, now dance
I am rhythmic tic 'o time
One among many

Relinquished of the vigor,
the vital, of my spring
Replenished in greater meaning
This is Love
One among many

I am the grass root.

The heron's in the dirty pond again,

William Seaton

The heron's in the dirty pond again,
and finds it very much a place of grace.
what with the turtles' gaze and trill of wrens
and churn of carp, a wet and homey place,
till into Eden comes a sudden hawk,
or twist of guts, unlooked-for fainting spell,
and then plot thickens, verities shake free,
and rises up mortality's old smell
with mystery of what is to be.
A little fish or froggy bit's enough
to take that far horizon from the eyes
and even if her call is a rash bluff,
it worked, and works, and will work till she dies.
And so we play a hero, villain, and the clown
and look this way and that till night comes down.

Breath of Spring, June 2023

Jim Seegert

I'll speak of—
No daffodils in the dew.
No robins in the park.
No butterflies on the wing.
Nothing like that—nothing.
Under an oxide blanket of a retro 20th century-style rust belt sky, I sit in self-quarantine. The air quality index unhealthy and rising. An air purifier plugged in by my side as the AC hums during this cool/dry late spring day.
Will this be the new normal?
I drift off to sleep with random, scattered, stuffy-headed, dreams of past summers bouncing in my brain.
Memories of Cape Cod National Seashore and Truro Light buffeted by fresh breezes off the Atlantic floating by. Followed by a day trip on the opposite coast to the aromatic soft forest floor of Muir Woods. Nice. Tranquil. Refreshing.
A decision, made after several slices and a couple beers at the end of a long day to drive from San Francisco to Bolder, CO by dinner the next night, the ethers of leaded-gasoline exhaust in the thin high desert night air fueling my joy ride.
Then a thrilling cruise on the Cross Bronx Expressway after camping in the Catskills.
The diesel exhaust of the ferry crossing the Bay of Fundy on a beautiful calm day. Clouds of cigarette smoke curling through a murky blues dive in the industrial Midwest.
I float down into the National Air Shows, serene out on the Toronto Islands but smoky, gritty and loud in Cleveland, standing on the sweltering tarmac or along the freight car rails, so fitting for that town. I'm in a plume of caster oil smoke from a vintage Sopwith Camel at the Old Rhinebeck Aerodrome then the full stench of LaGuardia airport upon arrival home after a summer sojourn.

A cough jolts me out of this brain fog or maybe the notification on my phone warning that the air quality from Canadian wild fires has gotten worse—I should remain indoors, if at all possible.
I'm in. It stinks! I fish for my handkerchief. I spit up some phlegm.
Right now, I'd swap all those airy memories for one precious June experience:
That long slow-dance in Montreal underneath a crystal-clear sky with the stars sparkling above—[starry, starry night.]
I must be dreaming...

Invisible Burqa

Debbie Shave

Sunset was thirty minutes ago
but I set out for a walk
under a moon with skin like burnt pumpkin
who tilts her head
three-quarters to peer
as best she can
between strips of gray gauze,
the slow-moving clouds, which
cover-smother-uncover her face.

My legs are bare
and white. They gleam in the streetlights
that drop pale puddles of LED
on a long sidewalk that climbs
a hill with nothing but dark woods
to the left,
sporadic traffic on the road
far below.

A man approaches
face lit by his cell phone.
The crickets sing shrilly,
the tree frogs creak warnings.
But nothing happens
as we pass one another,
indifferent ghosts
on different paths.

I cross Chestnut Street
and a breeze flutters my hair,
cool fingers on an August scalp.
Passing the pizza place parking lot,
I inhale bready scents
when suddenly
headlights flare, spotlight me
pushing stray locks of blonde from my face.
But nothing happens
as I pass through harmless halogen
in search of a quieter block.

In a neighborhood now
where yellow porch lights ward doors
and windows glow
television blue
and everyone's attention is turned
inward.
I wish an old man, with a large flashlight
and larger dog
a good evening.
But except for his nod
and a wagging tail,
nothing happens.

As I circle the block
in denim shorts and concert t-shirt,
pass, again, the noisy pizza place,
step into the crosswalk,
where my silhouette flickers against
impatient headlights,

no one throws stones
at my exposed arms,
curses my uncovered head,
chides my nocturnal strides,
unchaperoned.

I am not leered at nor jeered at;
not arrested nor reported.

Above me, the pumpkin moon veils and unveils
at the whim of the clouds.
But I am blessed with all the choice in the world.

Just This One

Nancy Shih-Knodel

The line was quite long, and we were
waiting patiently to get in. I saw her from
a distance, working the line with little success,
a middle-aged woman with dark, curly hair,
wearing an old coat, stained and tattered,
her hands open like an empty cup.

Years ago, in a street market in Ecuador,
we were surrounded by young boys,
their upturned faces speaking of their need.
Our tour guide was adamant, emphasizing a
fundamental rule for beggars: turn away,
don't look them in the eyes, not a single centavo.

When the woman finally reached our group,
I reached over and handed her some folded
bills, which she took, and hurried away.
You can't save everyone, people keep telling me,
as a way of saying you shouldn't save anyone.
But what if you could help just this one

person, though the offer was a humble one,
the smallest of gestures? What if it lasted only
a moment? Minutes later, the woman returned
unexpectedly, looking up and down to find me,
opening her arms out like a fan to give me an
embrace, a memento of the gift we shared.

Beautiful Ripples
for Roberto Burl Marx

Gary Siegel

Beautiful ripples rhythm their way through poisoned waters.
They move through tall grasses, discolored.
And the closed eye lid of a snapping turtle crinkles, revealing dehydration.

And I love that turtle.
I am caressed by those ripples.
I grieve for those grasses.

I have agitated for better.
I have imagined bountiful ease.
I have clung to visions of preservation.

And when it does not seem as if it is to be
I wipe the tear
   and caress the damage.
Wipe the tear
   and love what is left.

Beauty is still found in damaged landscapes.
It can be embraced in the starving coyotes.
Winds ruffling their fur and the sinking sun reflecting in their eyes.

The land and the earth and all the beings upon it
were supposed to last immeasurably long.
But it looks like we must grieve this too.

Find me a priestess.
One with deep vision.
One who can assuage our wounds.

Late day sun radiates through speckled clouds
throwing shadow and light in swaying, moving shapes upon the ground.
Shapes which look strangely
like tears.

Grandma dreams

Nathan Smith

Grandma dreams in whispers
In smoky silhouettes of a world she once knew
Of the world we left behind
And all the moments passed since then.
Grandma dreams in technicolor,
Of the days in her youth before TVs had that sort of thing
She dreams of her favorite memories
The ones from many years ago
Some she can no longer speak about
Some you already know
And some from just last week
You see grandma dreams at 6pm
Before the sun has event set
Leaning back in grandpa's chair
Breathing in his distinctive scent
Though she knows he is gone
She tries not think about that now
Instead, grandma dreams of bowling alleys
The one where he took her on their first date
And all the times they'd gone together since then
And all the colors of the bowling balls
Their signature roll and tumble
The loud roar of the resin on waxed wooden floors
Like grandpa's laugh
She misses his laugh, his touch,
And as the ball hits the pins of her dreams she remembers his golfing days
Dragging her to the golf course every Thursday
Drinking coffee and watching flags blow in the wind as she cheered him on Though he never was much good at that sort of thing
But lord she would never say it to his face.
Watching ball after ball roll by the waving flags and giggling to herself
And as the ball dips into the earth,

she remembers the marbles her children used to play with
How she had taught them how to play
The games she learned when she was about their age
How did that game go again?
But they could never remember to pick them back up after they were done
Like the time grandpa stepped on the marbles
And dropped a whole tray of Christmas cookies that she had baked
Oh what was that recipe again?
He was so angry at first, but anger evolved into laughter which faded into love
And she remembers cleaning up the floors together and him hiding the marbles in her purse for her to find the next day so she could laugh about it all over again.
Oh I wonder where those marbles are now? Grandma dreams with the lights on
With grandpa's hat in her lap
About their first date at the golf course
Or maybe she taught him to play marbles?
She knows she is starting to forget
To lose steam and dreams
And as afternoon ticks away into dark
She just hopes she doesn't forget the man she first learned to dream about.
With the lights on.

The Beautiful Death Around Us

Megha Sood

Based on the invasive species, the lanternfly emerging in
the summer of 2022 in the Eastern part of the United States

I have been taught by my granny to always help an animal in need.
Even an insect, a monarch with broken wings
fluttering in the shining mud,
shining bravely in the apricity of the city—
stopping us in our tracks.

I hold it gently in the center of my soft palms, like an infant,
cuddling its existence with all my warmth
and tend to its broken wings till it can fly.

One day, a small-breasted warbler crashed against the blinding windows
of my high-rise and fell on the balcony.
Death is a shining thing. It draws you in, like a pied piper.
A shining penny half-covered in a roll of hay.

I tend to its broken wings and wait feverishly for it to open its eyes.
Numerous tales of kindness and humility come back to me rushing
when sometimes kindness becomes a stranger to me.

These days are strange. The year is strange—
Death and the dying have been given a new name.
The normal has been anointed again.

And yet again, there is an invasive species as beautiful as a
dream in the thicket of the night
with its spotted wings and fiery abdomen.

A spotted lanternfly. And the message that it brings for us is "When you see it, kill it."
What a terrible act of survival. It's either them or us.
The existence is beautiful and yet so devastating.

Sometimes I feel how much kindness is left inside this withering soul of mine, which can kill a living being with all my might.

Yesterday

Amanda Spadafino

the thing is, i didn't realize childhood has an expiration date
it's as easy as it is not to move from one day to the next
because the self-portrait i picture in my mind today
feels the same as my first

because when i look in the mirror
i feel in the deepest parts of my heart
the same as i did yesterday
and yesterday's yesterday, and the day before that

because all i know is this moment
until it has ripped edges and faded colors in a dust covered box
or home movies as close as the hand holding the camera
to touching hers as mine

but as distant as the static i can't quite see through
and as still as i feel in my eyes at this moment
vivid but fuzzy and just out of reach
nevertheless, i still go there like it was yesterday

i still walk through young eyes
with a lens that i can't quite get around
but somehow still feel the warmth in her soul
and the peace in her mind
that little girl i don't entirely recognize
but know i remember her as she'll find me now

and holding in my hands the flashes of what seems to be another life
so many yesterdays ago
i can't see it as well but i feel it
the way it was stored in safe keeping the first time

in the fullness of a second yesterday
and in the messy collection of everyday after's tomorrow
just the way she left it
to visit in the hearts of our minds on rainy days like today

Red Button

Matthew J, Spireng

The sticker on the front-loading washing machine
at the Laundromat says Push red button
before turning handle, but there is no red button
except the red button fallen from a garment

that I noticed on the floor, so maybe that's
the red button they mean, maybe
it's there on the floor for just that reason,
and maybe it's a magical button and I'm

the first who's noticed it and if I push it
and turn the handle it will open a door
to somewhere no one has been before,
and then what shall I do?

Predator

Lisa St. John

I'd catch prey, hold them toward the sky on a platter. I'd offer them to you, red-shouldered hawk: the chipmunks, snakes, and mice in my yard. Sometimes a rabbit. I'd hold them high enough for you to swoop down and take your pick.

I look up as you screeeee above me, your black and white tail fanned in flight. See your rich, red-brown belly and wonder about the hunt, about hunger.

Oh, if my eyes could see as yours do, but what do I have to see after all? Down here, we have cellophaned steaks. You don't need the mahEEP, mahEEP of the robin's warning call to see her nest is ripe.

Liminal Life

Victoria Sullivan

I press my nose to the screen and
not only see the rain, but feel it.
This is liminal life, on the porch,
neither in the house nor outside,
but something in-between,
with the rain and trees and
the darkening sky. Thunder
rumbles and I am part of the
storm. It is the life I choose,
living closer to nature, and
at night in bed on the porch,
I hear the feet of creatures
nearby, scuffling through the
leaves. We breathe the same
air, cross the species barrier,
inhabit this land like neighbors.

I live for these months when
I can sleep outdoors, when,
if the wind changes direction,
my bed may grow damp with rain.

I've grown tired of cities and sidewalks,
yearning to dine only on greenness
and sunshine, craving the melody
of wind and bird song, with the moon
light at night, like a benevolent lover,
dropping by at midnight to bathe
me in moon bliss. There is no
sweeter kiss.

And so my home is
neither in nor out, but a heartbeat
in-between, neither past nor future,
yet here – now – so briefly on planet earth,
vibrating to its sacred melody.

All Wars Are The Same

Victoria Sullivan

Beware the beauty of the beast,
the forest green, the heart corrupt.
Sit still and listen to the rain
while all around, the wounded cry.

This is the moment of pain,
souls caught in the nape of the storm.
Trees fall. Thunder cracks the sky,
and birds fly low, a mass of crows,
denuding the landscape as they go.

Nightmare scene: the old are crushed
by wagon wheels of flame. Surely it is war,
but what is the name of this barren
country, this crossfire zone, this tender
trap of death? You have cast off your
uniform, dropped your gun, and are
running through a field under
a barrage of artillery fire.

You hide behind an abandoned hut.
You pray as best you can, forgetting
the appropriate words, sobbing a little,
gasping for breath, your trousers
soaked with blood or urine.

You have run so far, you have run so fast.
You remember your mother crying
at the train station when you left for the front.
She wanted to touch your hair. You brushed
her hand away, I am a man, you said,
and she tried to stop crying. You waved
from the train window, and dreamt that
night of Lola, with her snow white thighs.
Now you are wounded and afraid you might
die, or never be able to sleep deeply again.

You've heard of shell shock. You imagine
going home, and it all seems impossible,
ever to sleep in a downy bed again, ever
to have mother bring you morning tea.
Now you are a man. It is a crushing blow.

The History of Jazz   **Finalist**

Tim Tomlinson

In the second edition
of Ted Gioia's monumental
The History of Jazz

the word Connecticut
appears only once
in five-hundred sixty-seven pages.

First edition, too.

There are reasons for this.

Adolescents of 1968

Tim Tomlinson

Some of us
carried Khalil Gibran,
some of us
Eldridge Cleaver.

We were all part
of the revolution.
The revolution
was against

our teachers,
our parents,
our politicians,
our institutions.

They won.

Word play

Daniel Villegas

I'm eating garlic on the side
without a heartache
Burned half of my kitchen down
This situation gets real
Like carnage
My bondage
I break slavery chains
With constant
Contact
Delivering
Folks
That combat
The mission
I slice mics precision
In half with more vision
Than cats
My 9 lives can match
Where ever your at
With an umpire
Holding the stats
My metaphors
Are sick
Like when catching a cold
Writing with bold
Italicized
Penmanship
All on the road
I'm touring the globe
And in it
I can see where to go

Punchlines
Hit hard
So get up from the floor
3 rings
With more strings being pulled from science
String theory
Dimensions
Are doors
To multiple realities
I canopy
With trees stretched out
Like the kennedies
Before John got shot
Put the gun down
We don't need to write out blocks
And I meant that
I write more than waterfalls
Catch that rock
On crops
That crop
Photos
To fit that block
on your phone
I ET phone home
Whenever I cyclone
My mind though
To unwind
The past yo
And never repeat
Mistakes
Are granted

I'm m holding a key
To and unlocked box
I called it hip hop whenever I beat box
So plant yourself
To the ground and speculate
How many more times does it take you
To interface
My reality
Of word play
My words say
Don't worry
The people will come
So for now I kick this rhyme
For the people above

Word Play

The Next Time I Fall In Love

George Wallace

The next time I fall in love the earth will resume its shaking, the electricity of your hand in mine will shock and dismay, yet I will be solid as a heavyweight in the early rounds, rock steady on my feet, possessor of all the punch a young man may deliver or take blow from, confident in my stride, the next time I fall in love,

No drowse in my step no foot-dragging no drunken fool, no noises to distract me, I will be done with all that and the sweetness of your strawberry kisses will redden these lips again and the gods will blind me as pleasantly as the gods may do, and the breath of your mouth in mine will render me senseless;

Fresh as fresh kill in the rift valley, prostrate in the sun,

And I will be the relentless one, though humbled, though pulled down by the lioness and slaughtered like a Serengeti gazelle, rendered, not rendering, undeterred, grasping for the insane rescue, unclothed, casualty to the treasure and truth that has always rested beyond the fingertips of love;

The next time I fall in love having entered this ring before and been true to my calling and gored for my pain I will dwell no wiser, stand sure as the sparks falling around me, the impetuous one at the carnival, the amplifier, the reckless one, guided by the primary senses of love, I will fall in love all right;

This is my pledge and my plea, though a different sun rise altogether to my sight, though circumstances change; I will observe the same custom and rite, Dionysian; my head will heave heavenward with the same strange energy and disarray, I will plunge deep into the deep, dagger-like into it -- though my heart's blood cry, though my breast say wait, though the winds of temperance pass across my furious body in vain attempt to subdue me.

The Object Of My Desire

George Wallace

because life was so much younger and full of surprises back in the tenderloin years and the girl from my bible school was all grown up and stood six foot tall to a Colorado mountaintop and was magnificent, soft as the bossa nova and sweet as a cloud and wore a pink parka when she came back home from college

and it was snowing out and I heard her telling lies and making promises and everybody who didn't go to college expected to get drafted and I figured before I got shot in Vietnam I'd let

sex drugs and rock and roll do their thing with me

it was liberation and a lifeline to freedom

and I wanted to stick it to the man before the man stuck it to me so I took the old pike road to Boston, in my father's Oldsmobile, where her college was, parked the car near the Combat Zone, walked through the dogshit and icy rain, crowded through a turnstile and found my way to the back of the bar and stood there in the dark

shaking like a nervous puppy that had been leashed to a parking meter and somehow

slipped its collar and doesn't know what to do about it

and I watched her work her stuff on stage for the crowd, feeling dirty ashamed and blue,

feeling neglected and stupid, her not even knowing I was there, my fist in my pocket, tight as an unripe plum,

ready to fight any man
who stood between me and
the object of my desire

Convalescence

Bruce Weber

when i was growing up my fingers throbbed from turning so many pages. the weight of a tale of two cities almost crushed me. the nurses were pleasant. the doctors made me promise to embrace sleep as an ally but i read under the cover of night with my flashlight devouring the arabian nights and tales of the brothers grim. i danced around the truth till the truth waltzed away shyly. defending myself from the sheepish questions of lovers by reading till dawn crept under the door quiet as a lamb. the convalescence was sweet. a victory for my fingers and my soul. i charted the wonders of every page like a merchant adding up sous while butterflies sprinted across the garden like mcabees. playing tag with sparrows. pole vaulting petunias and bee balms. anticipating the whir of the engine and the tumult of turning gears chomping on grass. the butterflies disappeared after that summer. a pall was cast over their beauty that stung. the endless days of pouring rain drowned everything. even emily dickinson's poems couldn't keep the butterflies in tow. the falling of summer on their delicate skin, breaking the thread of their conversation with the sun. a sudden thud on the roof of all that happened that summer while my fingers silently healed.

it was just another weekend in 1885
for mick

Bruce Weber

it was just another weekend in 1885 and i was feeling flush with the dazzling light of the impressionists. my mind gyrated in small circles like dots on a canvas. anticipating the flurry of a thick snow storm falling on notre dame or the maddening penchant for evenness in a sky by the boy wonder georges seurat. sometimes i would get lost in a mauve shadow under the hoof of a carriage horse or begin to vibrate like a checkerboard tabletop or whiz by like a carrier pigeon delivering messages from rodin to his mistress sophie. sometimes i would go down by the quay near the boulevard maupassant and spin cartwheels for centimes or balance atop the thin wall dividing life and a death roll into the river seine. in the tulleries monet greeted us with a bouquet of violet flowers or doffed his top hat in perfect imitation of the bougoisie. renoir would pinch the roundness of one or two of his models and then slink off to the bar for some absinthe. and degas' little ballerina would sometimes pirouette into the day like a trick fly on a string making us reach for air every time she cried or coughed or opened her mouth to sing. yes it was just another weekend in 1885 and i was heading off in the white and blue and gray impasto of the speeding train to my cottage in argenteuil.

John Lennon

Dan Wilcox

Shoes full of snow on the window sill
like riderless horses at funerals
empty boots backwards in the stirrups

& barefoot Beatles on the album cover
alive then, the other one died
years later — we're never sure
what these prophecies mean.

The Glass Studio

2nd place

Sandra Yannone

In the Copper Room in Limerick, on what should be called Copper
Road, the low copper ceiling is held up by copper walls. They sing me

their copper songs whenever I can be within them under copper
ground. Last visit, Edward and I drank pint after coppery pint

of Treaty Ale, so many coppery pints that we began to see
our reflections in our makeshift hall of copper mirrors; another night,

another friend told me about her cancer but didn't use that word,
choosing instead to call it something more shimmery or burnished

like copper, while the candles amplified their messages
against the copper walls. The Copper Room always feels familiar

like the press of copper foil between my fingers
that I used to wrap pieces of hand-cut glass in my father's stained

glass studio as a girl. Every now and then the copper foil
would slice through my unsuspecting skin; my blood would ooze

like a copper river until someone would bandage me,
the blood drying to an even deeper, copper hew. Every lamp

in the studio was made that way: copper foil, silver solder,
a toxic elixir of patina that muted the shine. People

would buy their lamps to hang in their copper kitchens
near their copper pans, but few knew the process to make

each lamp as I did. Few know that copper lay buried
beneath the skin of the solder's seams or of all that blood

turned copper that went into the making of their coppery light.

The Brotherhood of Sleeping Car Porters
    for Kabby Mitchell III, (1956-2017)

Sandra Yannone

At the Quality Inn off Aurora
and John, I greet an elder brother
with a particular train cap on his head,

a Pullman porter whose stepped out of time
while we wait to ride the elevator with my grief
and gratitude and whatever else he has brought

from his travels. I can see how he punches
tickets, memorizes routes and timetables
in the way he cares for me in this moment.

I tell him about you. The elevator
opens. We step in. We rise up
the spine of the hotel. And even though it's just

the Quality Inn, nothing ornate or special or flashy,
I think about how this unadorned Seattle box
might transform into Charlie's Great Glass Elevator

and take me to the highest floor of the sky
just to be with you a bit longer, knowing
I would need to return, and not entirely sure

why the divine chose this timetable
at this appointed hour on this particular day
nestled inside this week tucked inside this year

during this crazed century. Kabby, at the Primo Grill
two weeks ago on my last night before leaving
for Limerick, we flirted at the bar with disaster,

you reluctantly, when I suggested that I might not
see you again if fate would choose to take me away.
You, wide-eyed, incredulous, almost scolding.

So I returned, and now you are gone. Strange.
It will take the rest of my strange life
to get used to this estrangement,

like meeting a train porter
in front of a modest Quality Inn elevator
who steps off on my floor

and leads me down the hall
to his hotel room door, stands there with me
for half an hour reciting from John:1,

imploring me to consider how I am here
and that you are now everywhere
as you always have been

with your moonlit eyes and
incandescent smile. He stands there,
a train porter on break, no stranger to me

than a stranger I feel ready to know
like the first time I met you two days after 9/11
while we ate a catered chicken lunch

from the Southern Kitchen in Tacoma,
your hospitality that day never lost to me
after all these years. He stands there

 in front of that Quality Inn door, room 223,
never inviting me in. The train porter
just opens his wallet, removes his business

card, writes something on the back,
and hands it to me as if it were a train ticket receipt
and sends me down the hall to find my room

where I fall into my feathered bed, sleep
hard and wake to the day's breaking
news of your leaving spreading across time

and these cities you've inhabited like a love train
not entirely desperate to stay true
to its scheduled departure.

Later, back on campus in Olympia,
my students and I marvel at the unannounced
thunder for a full two hours. There is nothing else

we can do after the emergency alert system
promises hail. We wait. The hail does not come.
My students turn in their reflections for the week

slightly disappointed. They leave.
I walk across campus alone almost
taking a detour to your office

then drive home through the city expecting
your lightning to strike me dead.
And I admit that I almost wish for this

lightning bolt strike rather than make it home
safely to go to bed only to wake
to my first day without you, wondering

whether grace can find me if I'm not at the Quality Inn
in Seattle on John Street with train porter Brother Will
from Breaking Bread Ministries

looking out for me looking everywhere for you.

Finalist

Glenn Werner

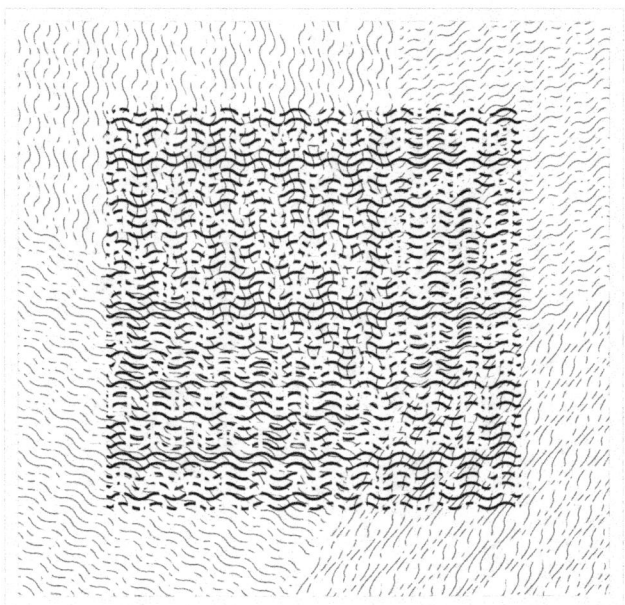

Concrete Ekphrasis: 25 Wide Pantoum

COLOR FORM TONE LINE SYLLABLE
RESPONSIVE AS TO COMPOSITION
OF ALPHABETIC GRAPHEME UNITS
ARRANGED TOWARD SET PURPOSES

RESPONSIVE AS TO COMPOSITION
RADIAL CONSTRUCTS AND RHYTHM
ARRANGED TOWARD SET PURPOSES
WEAVE INTO THE PROSODIC FIELD

RADIAL CONSTRUCTS AND RHYTHM
DRAW SCAFFOLDS INTO SUBJECTS
WOVEN INTO THE PROSODIC FIELD
OF A DISTINCT AGGREGATE VOICE

THE DRAWN SCAFFOLD IS SUBJECT
TO ALPHABETIC GRAPHEME UNITS
OF DISTANT AGGREGATED VOICES
COLOR FORM TONE LINE SYLLABLE

In Memoriam

Bob Barci, grew up in Elmont, NY. He graduated from Windham College where a creative writing class inspired his life-long interest in poetry. Most of his poems are short and deceptively simple in language, but express the joyful feelings of wonder, the deep satisfaction derived from everyday experiences, and the timelessness of love and friendship.
A mainstay on the Manhattan poetry scene, his emotionally charged works earned him the nickname, "Mr. Untitled.

Bluejay

I found myself alone today,
    with a bluejay that had died, yesterday.
The cat had played a vicious game
    that left the bird in this altered state.
The bird now flies among the stars
    searching for a place to rest his feet.

I found myself alone today,
wondering if that bluejay
will find its place to rest.
Perhaps someday I'll fly with that bird.

Bluejay, you're welcome to rest upon my shoulder.
Join me on a flight of my own
    as we make our way through this universe.
When and if you should leave me,
    keep in mind our flight together
    and this altered state
    won't seem so bad.

Saul Bennett (1936-2006) released two collections in his lifetime, *New Fields and Other Stones* and *Harpo Marx at Prayer*, after being "shocked" into poetry, as he would say, by the sudden death of his daughter at twenty-four. Grief was his great subject — he'd also lost both parents while in his early twenties — yet he treasured his memories of growing up in Sunnyside, Queens in the 1940s. After a career in public relations, he retired to Woodstock with his wife, wrote poems in his studio shed, published them in journals, and participated in the Woodstock Poetry Society. On Sunday mornings he could often be heard presenting local poets on WDST's Woodstock Roundtable. His death was sudden and mourned by many. But his poetry lives on.

Untitled

I loved learning William Carlos Williams
interned at the Manhattan hospital
where decades after I was born;

— feeling him feeling his way
around rounds there, watching him tip-
toe out of Mother's room-to-be with me;

— imagining on his way out
he had a poem notion, scratched it down there,
then, distracted, dropped his scrap;

— dreaming it undiscovered there,
implanted, invisible over time
inside a baseboard crack;

(loving, but not so much, because it happens
all the time, William wondering
where in hell his fragment fell.)

— believing Mother about to depart
chased her fallen eyebrow pencil
to the leaking crack, spotted scrap, knelt there;

— observing Mother dropping
Williams into her purse
before a Checker brought us three and Father home;

— pretending 40 years after his death,
nodding over Mother's keepsakes,
exhuming the faded, inked jumble;

— decrypting this skeletal poem,
ascribing those bones irrefutably to Williams,
thanks due Mother, who routinely rescued small things.

—Fom the unpublished manuscript Sea Dust by Saul Bennett. Courtesy Will Nixon.

In addition to a long career as an instructor in Tri-Valley Central Schools, Barbara Boncek (1930-2023) was an active member of both The Alchemy Poetry Club of Grahamsville NY and the Stone Ridge Poetry Society. A painter as well as a writer, her poetry was published in Outloud, Oxalis Literary Quarterly, Almanac, and Stone Ridge Poetry. Her book, *The World of Soft Edges* was published by Crazy Ladies Press, 2001.

Rain Walk

They tell me
> I was born in a hayfield
> just as the storm broke
> and my first comfort was not
> the arms of my mother
> but a bath of warm rain
> that washed me clean of birth.

They tell me
> my father wrapped me
> in his sweat-wet bandana
> and brought me to the house
> leaving me on the cool parlor floor
> while he returned to the hayfield
> for my rain-soaked mother
> whose moans forced him to leave us
> in search of a doctor.

They tell me
> as sick as my mother was
> she tried to comfort me
> by stripping away the bandana
> and wrapping me in a rag rug
> and between the sobs
> she hummed lullabies
> until I fell asleep.

I do not tell them
  that my night dreams
  are full of sobs
  that when a summer storm breaks
  I walk in its warm rain
  humming lullabies.

Originally published in Oxalis #18, 1992

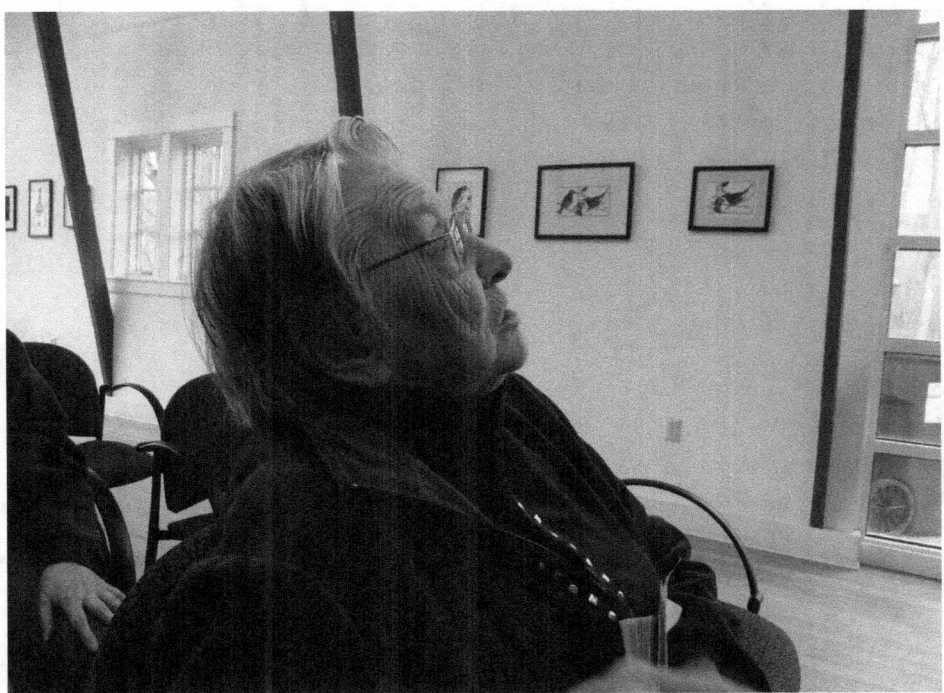

Frank Boyer started writing with the goofy idea of "becoming a writer" when he was 20 years old. The idea gave some sort of focus to his ongoing mania, as he bounced here and there, scattering himself across the landscape. He has been writing ever since, one way or another.

Landing in New York City in the late 1970's to pursue an interest in dance and performance, he stuck around for 15 years that spanned the 1980's. He participated in the performance art scene of the Lower East Side, collaborating with the normal bunch of lunatics, performing at PS122, LaMama, and other funky-chic venues. Occasionally he ventured uptown of 14th Street, usually to go to an art museum or catch a poetry reading, or to work at one of the legion of ludicrous jobs he took to support his art habit.

In the late 1980's, when he was an artist in residence at Tompkins Square Library, he began to build installations using found objects and "talismans" from his past. He taught visual and performing arts-related subjects at SUNY-New Paltz and SUNY-Ulster. He had recently published a chapbook, *Jumping Out of My Skin*, and was working on a second one.

Street Blues

Outside my window
passing trains
play heart-ache harp.
A cold wind strums
the telephone lines,
fretting fingers
cross to cross.
Down the street
the traffic sings
street blues sweet blues.

In my attic room
I finally feel at home.

The Secret

Translated from the Spanish of the Bolivian Poet, Francisco de Campo, 1938

I wrote and addressed
a letter to my uncle.

I told him:
"The newspapers
are spreading the news rapidly."

I told him:
"The great and secret influence you exert
among the politicians
and the other criminals,
together with your money--
not to mention your sincere enthusiasm--
all these convince many of our people."

"You know," I said "I'm following
your advice."

To my uncle I wrote this letter.

I sent it to him with the leg
of a black widow spider
embalmed in a drop
of candle wax,
crushed flat between my thumb
and the first finger of my left hand,
then hidden
in an inside corner
of an innocent envelope.

It's time for moving on.

Enid Dame, (1943-2003) cofounded with her husband Donald Lev the HOME PLANET NEWS, was born in Beaver Falls PA. While dividing their time for many years between Brooklyn and High Falls NY, Dame also taught writing at Rutgers University and NJIT. She died on Christmas Day 2003.

"Lilith and The Woman Who Was Water" published in *Lilith & Her Denons* (Woman Writers Chapbook Series : No 2, 1989)

Lillith

kicked myself out of paradise left a hole in the morning
no note no goodbye
the man I lived with was patient and hairy
he cared for the animals worked late at night planting vegetables
under the moon
sometimes he'd hold me our long hair tangled he kept me from rolling off
the planet
it was always safe there but safety
wasn't enough. I kept nagging pointing out flaws in his logic
he carried a god around in his pocket consulted it like
a watch or an almanac
it always proved
I was wrong
two against one isn't fair! I cried and stormed out of Eden into history:
the Middle Ages were sort of fun they called me a witch
I kept dropping
in and Out
of people's sexual fantasies
now
I work in New Jersey take art lessons live with a cabdriver
he says: baby
what I like about you is your sense of humor
sometimes
I cry in the bathroom remembering Eden and the man and the god
I couldn't live with

An early supporter of Calling All Poets, Lew Gardner (1943-2020) wrote plays, fiction, nonfiction, and verse for several decades. A number of his one-act plays can be ordered from One Act Play Depot. His "Pete & Joe at the Dew Drop Inn" is included in Best American Short Plays 2008-2009. More than 60 examples of his poems and light verse have been published in the New York Times.

In the Garden of the Senior Residence

Jean tells how she'd go to pubs
and meet American soldiers--she'd sing
the latest songs--White Cliffs of Dover,
Berkeley Square--teenager in London
in the war years, time of privation,
of jokes in the bomb shelter. She tells us
in the fading light, surrounded
by wings of the building.
Every night, after feeding all
her younger brothers and sisters (mother
dead, her father an alcoholic),
out she'd go--it was a wonderful
time--"Sing us another one, Jeannie!"--
as well as a terrible time--"The boy
you danced with could be dead
the next week," she says.
We hear a siren beyond the garden
walls--a resident rushed to the hospital.
An American married Jean, brought her
to Massachusetts; when he beat her,
she had to leave him. A nanny in Boston,
raising other women's children--
when the husband died, her sons
began to visit her.
Tears in her eyes as we speak--there's
a new director of the residents' choir

who won't let Jean sing solos,
so she's quit the choir. "My heart
isn't in it anymore. They all
like my songs--I know the words
of all the old songs--but she
doesn't want me to sing them."
Sing for us, I ask, sing
White Cliffs of Dover. "Here?" she asks.
"Here and now?" Please, I say,
and she sings--her light, clear soprano
reminding us of bright nights
when life was waiting for everyone young
to bite huge chunks and down them with beer
before the sirens wailed.

An early and ardent supporter of Voices of the Valley and CAPS, Lynn Hoins, (d. 2021) was published in journals including Earth's Daughters, Inkwell, Chronogram, and cine sera. Her two chapbooks, both published by Finishing Line Press were *You Were Always Music* and *Called by Stones*. She taught poetry workshops for The College of Poetry of The Northeast Poetry Center, Warwick, New York. She featured and read at open mics in New York State and Utah.

A Villanelle for Kathryn, The Pilot's Wife *

> The hearts breaks and breaks
> and lives by breaking.
> It is necessary to go
> through dark and deeper dark
> and not turn.
>
> - Stanley Kunitz from "The Testing Tree"

One must not turn from the dark to deeper dark.
The heart must break and break and live by breaking.
One needs to die before one can embark.

This time is velvet, deep and very stark
'til one has mastered loss, the art of aching.
One must not turn from the dark to deeper dark

to hear. on wind that voice that once said, "Hark,
come be my love; it's yours now for the taking."
One needs to die before one can embark.

And as one's soul is left without a spark,
one drinks the. draught of sorrow overtaking. . .
One must not turn from the dark to deeper dark

to look for help, to run from blackest mark
of one who promised much, before forsaking.
One needs to die before one can embark

As mended flies the broken winged lark —
she sings her joy, she sings he. re-awaking.
One must not turn from the dark to deeper dark;
one needs to die before one can embark.

"The Pilot's Wife" is a novel by Anita Shreve. Kathryn Lyons is the protagonist whose husband, a pilot, is killed in a plane crash.

Originally published in the CAPS Poetry 2015 Anthology (CAPS Press, 2015)

Born in Kingston NY, Lei Isaac's parents were residents of the Maverick Arts Colony in Woodstock NY. Lei Isaacs' first byline was in the Woodstock Press at age 12. She continued to work as a journalist and passionate animal rights activist her entire life. She died in 2021. She read many, many times for Calling All Poets.

CRUCIFIXION

"Hold his hand down," I told her
"While I get this brad into his feet."
Devout second-generation pantheist and reborn macrobiotic
    Buddhist, she quailed.
"Oh, come ON," I said. "It isn't like it hasn't
happened before."
(Actually, the antique crucifix I got at a yard sale
Was perforated with nail holes
But Jesus, resolute on resurrection, or at least bungee-jumping
    without the cords
Kept leaving his wooden cross hanging on the wall while he plunged
head-first into the cat-box or the radiator.)
Jesus was brass and he was one heavy sucker.
Well, I had some two-inch brads that ought to
anchor him
(Barring miracle or termites.)
"I'm NOT going to hold Jesus down while you nail
him to the cross, " she said.
"He wouldn't mind," I said.
"Like, if he was going to get bent behind it, don't you think
    he would have done something about it 2000 years ago?"
"Like, maybe he did," she said.
So, if you ever see this brass Jesus,
Trussed out on the cross with an elastic band and
two lengths of gift-wrap ribbon,
Don't ask.
Our Father, who art in bondage,
Give me patience. Give me strength.
Give me the duct tape.

Born in New York City in 1936, Donald Lev attended Hunter College, worked in the wire rooms of the wire rooms of the Daily News and New York Times. Then drove a taxi cab for 20 years (with a 6 year hiatus in which he ran messages for and contributed poetry to, The Village Voice and operated the Home Planet Bookshop on the Lower East Side). His earliest poems appeared in print in 1958 and he started his first small press magazine, *HPN Anthology,* in 1969, the same year his brief underground film acting career pinnacled with his portrayal (he wrote his own lines) of the Poet in Robert Downey Sr.'s classic *Putney Swope*. He met Enid Dame (1943-2003) at a N.Y. Poets' Cooperative meeting in 1976. They became life partners in 1978, and in 1979 founded the literary tabloid *Home Planet News,* which Donald worked on till his passing in 2018.

Friend, mentor and supporter of poets everywhere and CAPS in particular, it is fair to say we all owe him a huge thank you and a round of applause.

Christopher Wheeling

A DISTURBANCE IN THE CROWD

A crowd had begun to gather early,
Typically Republican, with lots
Of blue haired granny types,
Waiting in front of the Queens Borough Hall
For the appearance of 1952 Republican
Presidential candidate Dwight David Eisenhower.

I was there too, sixteen years old, a volunteer for Adlai Stevenson,
Standing way back by the sidewalk, along with other volunteers
From our storefront headquarters directly across Queens Boulevard.

We were holding signs querying the candidate as to
What he'd do regarding this or that issue.
That was our total demonstration.
I began to sense a disturbance in the crowd.
It seemed to be directed at me.
"There's one of 'em now!" One of those
Blue haired grannies was declaiming, her sweet
Cookie giving features now contorted and hideous,
"There's one of them damn Jew commies!"
And all of a sudden a mob of Republicans
Came at me to rip my sign away
Which is the only personal damage I recall

Except a lifetime distaste for crowds.

Born in Ohio during The Great Depression, Shirley Powell came to Manhattan in 1971. Her first book of poems, *Parachutes*, came out in 1975. In the following year she compiled and published Womansong from a Women's Liberation reading at NYU. She hosted The Village Poetry Workshop and, in 1981, began Stone Ridge Poetry Society. With several area poets, she formed The Catskill Caravan, traveling through the metropolitan area and New England, spreading imagery through poetry readings. In 1981, her novel *Running Wild,* was published by Avon Books. She and her longtime partner Mildred Barker began Crazy Ladies Press in 1999.

Shirley was an early advocate and supporter of both Voices of the Valley and Calling All Poets.

Uncovered

Since surgery I'm getting used to
nakedness: my own belly's bulge
fragile skin resiliency of flesh

this wrinkly marvel

Reminded of a trip years ago
with mother and mother's mother
how
returning to motel suite
I found them naked
pale giggling girls
running through the rooms

Previously published in Oxalis, 1990

Pamela Twining (1951-2023) traveled the US with her partner, poet Andy Clausen, performing her work in California, Colorado, New York City, Michigan, Wisconsin and places in between. Her work has appeared in *Big Scream, Big Hammer, PoetryBay, The Café Review, Napalm Health Spa,* and *Heyday!*, among others. With Clausen, she co-curated "The Invisible Empires of Beatitude" page at The Museum of American Poetics (www.poetspath.com) and for several years, she co-produced the Janine Pommy Vega Poetry Festival in Woodstock, NY. She is author of four chapbooks, "*i have been a river…*"(2011), "*utopians & madmen*" (2012), "*A Thousand Years of Wanting; the Erotic Poetry of Pamela Twining*" (2013) and "*Renegade Boots*" (2019).

The Cave

return to light
eyes blinded after darkness
       impenetrable
it's just too much all at once
greedy. pupils expand / contract
will the images fade
like photographs
       overexposed?

return to light
return to water after starvation/
thirst
troglodyte climbing
climbing from the bowels of the earth
the eyes have not gone useless
yet

electric blue gaze of heaven
       paralyzing
teach me again
to behold the universe

from i have been a river . . . Selected Poems (Dancing Fool Press, 2011)

Pauline Uchmanowicz (1957-2019) is the author of the poetry colletion *Starfish* (Twelve Winters Press, 2016) as well two poetry chapbooks; she received residency grants at the MacDowell Colony and Yaddo. She joined the English Department faculty at SUNY New Paltz in 1996, received tenure in 2002 and was promoted to full professor in the spring of 2019. Pauline served as Coordinator of the Composition Program and Director of the Creative Writing Program. She nurtured many aspiring student authors and ushered numerous writers, in particular poets, into print as an Associate Editor at Codhill Press.

Elements of Style

What if poets had to pick? The ocean or the stars.
A reputation in truth telling or a prize in diplomacy?

Seabed or zodiac. Water or fire. Density or infinity.
There's travel by Chinese junk with shipwreck

Or space capsule disaster. Commerce or exploration.
Marine biologist, aeronautic engineer.

Dictating rhyme, form and meter it's either
Waves as repetition or constellations as pattern,

Tide and undertow or equinox and quasar.
Cardinal points and horizon stay in joint custody

 And every bard gets clarinets, trees and the rigadoon.
Also Spanish butterflies, mountains and Dutch windmills.

Previously published in Starfish (Twelve Winters Press 2016)

Janine Pommy Vega (1942-2010) was a rare female comrade of the Beat Poets of the late 1950's/early 1960's. Janine traveled around the world writing and teaching her exuberant style of verse. She taught in New York prisons through the Bard Prison Initiative. She read in the late 1990's for Voices of the Valley, the poetry program that folded into Calling All Poets in 2003.

The Green Piano first published in *The Green Piano* (Black Sparrow Books, 2005)

The Green Piano: I
    for Bill Heine

When silence falls in the dining room it's the green piano:
someone has lifted the lid and begun to play
dancers land
serious players lean their heads to the left
a year compressed into a single rest stop barely touches the pedals
a pulse like elastic bands contracts and stretches the dancer's calf muscles, a player
raises her hands above the keyboard meteor showers in Gemini play all night long
no frog jumps in, no water sound statues in the town square surge miraculously forward, distant footsteps divide the stillness into bites, the walker never arrives the streaming helmets wear velocity
in the barely fluted edges
Opinions are divided
between full moon and empty moon
Which best purveys the empty space?
Which house is best for the Green Sonata?

   Willow, New York, January 2002

A son of the Bronx brought up in the hills of Mahwah, Ron Dionysius Whiteurs lived in the Ulster County area since 1966. With an MA from SUNY New Paltz, he taught English at that institution in 1970-71. Whiteurs' work has been published in *Arabesque, Home Planet News, Chronogram, Hunger, The Rondout Review,* and the Swiss journal *Wuzz Buzzin*. Never content with the printed page alone, he has slammed at the Nuyorican, featured at the Outloud Festival, and performed at the Byrdcliffe Barn as part of Summerjazz. Ron's poetry was a heady mix of bard and bawdy.

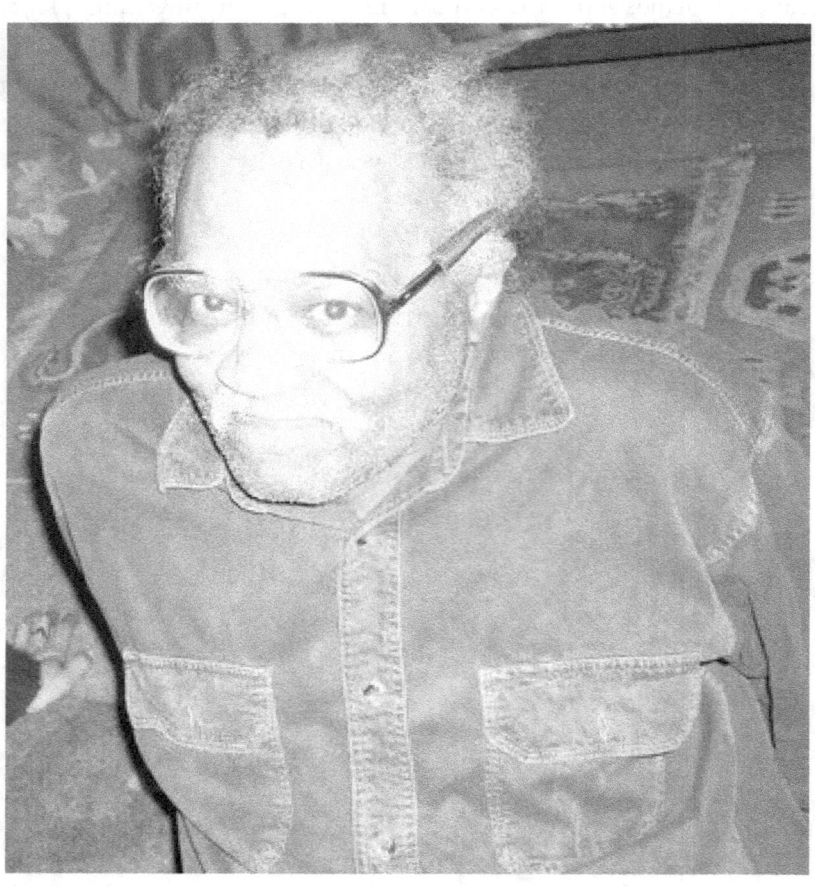

Shofar

Two
Living
Young
Kosher
Statuettes

Male
Warm, dense, dark
Apollonian locks
In natural, close-set rivulets;
Close-set eyes, as well,
With tragic spells.

Ah, those eyes, those lips
    those thighs, those hips,
Such liveliness, such earnestness!

Implanted on collegiate corner
Wrapped in animate conversation
Oblivious
To my intimately prying concentration:
At once
I am cantor, shofar, Psalter, psalm, and mourner.

In his own words, Ralph Villano was Artist + Photographer + Sculptor + Shaman + Mercenary +?; Seer, Seeker, Cynic, Sinner, and Very, Very, Very Occasionally Saint. Iconoclastic Misanthropic Malcontent with Subversive Tendencies. Autodidactic Polymath. Miner and Minder of Men's Souls. Wonderer and Wanderer. Neo-Luddite Libertarian Anarchist Ne'er-do-well and Rogue. Rebel/Deviant/Poet. Hard Sharp Mind. Intuitive Broad-Based Parallel Polytheistic Breadth of Knowledge, and Way of Thinking. Have Gun, Will Travel. His chapbooks, all published by Handmade Books, include *The Things I've Seen, Smoke This Book, yes I am an annoying bastard*, and all of them. Villano died in 2021 at 57.

Meditation on the Zen of Falling

Be still.
Find your center.
Push off.

Give yourself to the cut.
Hoka Hey.

Yes.
It is a good day to die.
The Lakota knew.
To be in the center.
When you throw your body out of an airplane at 16,000 feet,
It gets your undivided attention.
You cannot think of anything else
except the present.
You are there, you are seated to the moment.
Something will happen in a minute or two and you will handle it.
Different and the same every time.
Have you ever drempt that you could fly? You can, you know.
The human body has the same glide ratio as the Space Shuttle.
Though
landings are a bit harder.

Don Yacullo, musician, writer, naturalist, and humanitarian. He worked for the Kingston City School for Boys for fifteen years and the Saugerties School District for twenty one years.

The Poets

Roger Aplon, has published thirteen books: Most recently: *Mustering What's Left – Selected & New Poems – 1976 – 2017* from Unsolicited Press. He lives in Beacon, N Y & publishes the poetry magazine: *"Waymark – Voices of the Valley."* You can read and hear examples of his work at: rogeraplon.com

Catherine Arra is the author of four full-length poetry collections and four chapbooks. Her newest work is *Solitude, Tarot & the Corona Blues* (Kelsay Books, 2022) A Pushcart nominee, Arra lives in upstate New York, where she teaches part-time and facilitates local writing groups. Find her at www.catherinearra.com

Deyva is: photographer, writer, mother, activist, child, lover, forever trying to understand. She has received awards for her writings and photography of the human story. Deyva has been a journalist, artist, editor, housing organizer, environmental researcher, counselor for refugees, the mentally ill, and the homeless, a secretary, construction worker, and sheep farmer.

Amy Barone's poetry collection, *Defying Extinction*, was published by Broadstone Books in 2022. New York Quarterly Books published her book, *We Became Summer*. She wrote chapbooks *Kamikaze Dance* (Finishing Line Press) and *Views from the Driveway* (Foothills Publishing.) Barone belongs to the Poetry Society of America. She lives in NYC.

John Bartell is, somehow, the president of the Fort Worth Poetry Society. You can find his poetry in journals such as *The Orchards Poetry Review, Canyon Voices, The Loch Raven Review, Rat's Ass Review, Blue Hole Poetry Anthology* and *Muddy River Poetry Review*.

Rachel R. Baum is a Best of the Net nominated poet. She is the editor of *Funeral and Memorial Service Readings Poems and Tributes* (McFarland, 1999). Her poems have appeared in The Phare, Raven's Perch, and many others. In Dreams Cars Flew: poems will be published by Dancing Girl Press.

Eddie Bell is a free-verse poet whose writings focus on the Black experience of yesterday and today, as well as his renderings of nature and societal observations. Eddie's current projects are his fifth book of poetry, *Undulations*, and his first YA novel, *Cleo the Rail Rat*.

Naomi Bindman's work has appeared in *Mothering, So to Speak, Friends Journal, Consilience, Import Sky, Honeyguide, Lightwood, South Florida Poetry Journal,* and *First Literary Review*—East. She won Dogwood's 2023 Creative Nonfiction Award, has received Vermont Arts Council grants and taught memoir-writing workshops funded by the Vermont Humanities Council.

Mark Blackford has had poetry appear most recently in *Black Fox Literary Magazine, Oyez Review,* and *High Shelf Press*. Prior work has been nominated for a Pushcart, but nothing too recent. He read poetry once as an opener for Arlo Guthrie, on a strictly volunteer basis. He lives in Bushkill, Pennsylvania.

Marianna Boncek is an author, scholar, and researcher. Her latest novel *Diamond City* was published in 2023. Her poems and short stories have been published in a wide variety of anthologies and journals. Her poem *"Bittersweet"* won the 2021 Stephen DiBiase prize for poetry. She is also a playwright and two of her works have been featured in the Hudson Valley Short Play Festival. She has more degrees than necessary which makes her generally too educated to be employable. She reads and writes Middle Egyptian hieroglyphs — another valuable job skill. She lives with her partner, Dave, in one of New York's most famous small towns.

Kim D. Brandon is a Poet/Artist/Activist. Her work was included in three 50IN50 stage performances, *Emotive Fruition's Came Back with A Clap Back, The Dream Catcher's Song, the Peregrine Journal* and many others. She was presented a citation for community service in Brooklyn. Kim is completing her first poetry collection.

R. Bremner has written of incense, peppermints, and the color of time in *International Poetry Review, Passaic Review, Paterson Literary Review, Jerry Jazz Musician, Climate of Opinion: Sigmund Freud in Poetry, Red Wheelbarrow, Brownstone Poets,* and nine books/chapbooks, including *Hungry Words* (Alien Buddha Press), and *Absurd* (Cajun Mutt Press).

Tim Brennan (3rd Place): A poet painter and woodworker, I've lived and worked in Providence, San Francisco, Brooklyn, and now New Paltz, NY, where I've been renovating an old house for almost thirty years with no end in sight. I am interested in language drawn from observation, outside sources (collage, ambient speech and sound, some chance operations) and the meditative interior, twisting and juxtaposing words and syntax to restart perception.

Penny Brodie's poems have appeared in CAP's anthologies and the Maverick's program guide. She has performed her jazzoetry at Quin's, The Falcon, Greenkill Art Gallery, Flushing Town Hall and Café Istanbul in New Orleans. She has been involved in jazz radio for over 20 years and currently is the host of "Mingus Moments" at Vassar College, WVKR 91.3FM. Penny is also a licensed Speech Language Pathologist with over 30 years of experience.

Daniel Brown is a retired Special Education Teacher who began writing poetry as a senior. He published his first collection *FAMILY PORTRAITS IN VERSE And Other Illustrated Poems* at the age of 72. Daniel has been included in Arts Mid-Hudson's 'Poets Respond To Art', co-curated a show of jazz paintings at Gallery 40 Poughkeepsie, NY and has been published most recently in *Jerry Jazz Musician* and *The Ekphrastic Review*.

David Capellaro, resident of Millerton NY studied mass communications at Emerson College, Boston, covering film, poetry, radio and photography. David has been writing poetry since childhood, and has been published in local area publications such as the Hudson Valley Chronogram, and reads his work regularly at various open mic. venues.

Patricia Carragon is the author of *Angel Fire* (Alien Buddha Press), *Meowku* (Poets Wear Prada), *The Cupcake Chronicles* (Poets Wear Prada), and *Innocence* (Finishing Line Press). Available on amazon.com. She is the Curator/editor-in-chief of Brownstone Poets, Brooklyn, NY

Alan Catlin has dozens of chapbooks and full-length books. Among the latest are *Exterminating Angels* and *How Will the Heart Endure?* (both from Kelsay Books) and Listening to the Moonlight Sonata (Impspired).

Lucia Cherciu is the author of six books, including *Immigrant Prodigal Daughter* (Kelsay Books, 2023) and *Train Ride to Bucharest* (Sheep Meadow Press, 2017), winner of the Eugene Paul Nassar Poetry Prize. Cherciu is a Professor of English at Dutchess Community College and served as the 2021-2022 Dutchess County poet laureate.

Susan Chute (1st Place) is a poet, librarian, bookbinder, and curator of Next Year's Words. She has published in the *CAPS 2020 anthology; La Presa; Lightwood; Shawangunk Review* and the *WVW Anthology 2015; Reflecting Pool: Poets and the Creative Process*, and on the blogs of NYPL and Women's Studio Workshop.

Samuel Claiborne is a poet, essayist, composer, musician and shamanic healer. His poems have been published and anthologized, including in Chronogram and the anthologies *Voices of the Valley* and *Riverine*. And yet, through a combination of disorganization and laziness, he remains implacably anonymous.

Cassandra Clarke, poet, life coach, and social activist, mixes the arts with human understanding to build relationships that create peace and greater community.

Paul Clemente was born and raised on the banks of the Hudson River. He is young enough to have missed Woodstock and old enough to recall the mothballed fleet of WWII ships floating in Haverstraw Bay. He is a scientist who spent his career with the NY State Department of Environmental Conservation. Now retired, he lives in Esopus NY with his wife and two sons. He has published one chapbook *Luncheonette* which contains twenty sonnets.

Chris Collins has been published in several Hudson Valley magazines, an anthology and national publications. His work has been published in Arts Mid-Hudson's and WAAM shows; in an anthology: *Mightier - Poets for Social Justice*; in a humanist web zine: *A Poetry-Lover's Guide To The World-Wide Web, Post-1950 & Writers in the Mountains*.

John Jack Jackie (Edward) Cooper is the creator of *These Are Aphorithms* (aphorithms.blogspot.com), author of *Ten* (Poets Wear Prada, 2012), *Ten ... More* (Poets Wear Prada, 2016), and translator of *Wax Women*, with French texts of the original poems by Jean-Pierre Lemesle (International Art Office: Paris, 1985). His work has appeared widely, in print and online. He lives in France.

Ruth Danon's fourth book of poetry is *Turn Up the Heat*, from Nirala Series. She has published widely in the US and abroad. She lives in Beacon, NY, where, as founder of the Live Writing Project, she writes and teaches. She curates literary events in the Hudson Valley and beyond.

Joann Deiudicibus teaches writing and poetry in New York's Hudson Valley. Her poems and articles about poetry appear in *WaterWrites, A Slant of Light, & Reflecting Pool* (Codhill Press), *The Comstock Review, Typishly, Poetry Quarterly, Stone Poetry Quarterly, Drifting Sands, The Shawangunk Review, Chronogram, Affective Disorder and the Writing Life* (Palgrave Macmillan). Ask her about true crime, cats, and confessionalism.

Lenny DellaRocca is founding editor and former publisher of *South Florida Poetry Journal*. Author of five poetry collections, and his work has appeared in *One, Slipstream, Nimrod, Seattle Rev., Laurel Rev., Fairy Tale Rev*, and others. Poems forthcoming in *Last Stanza Poetry Journal, Cimarron Rev* and *North Dakota Quarterly*. Interviewed by Grace Cavalieri for The Poet and The Poem on NPR and nominated for a Pushcart Prize. Invented the Epoem a new form on display at his new poetry journal, *Witchery* (embedded online at South Florida Poetry Journal).

Deborah DeNicola has published seven books, most recently *The Impossible*, from Kelsay Press. Others include *Original Human, Where Divinity Begins* and her memoir *The Future That Brought Her Here*. Deborah edited *Orpheus & Company*; poems on Greek Myth, and four chapbooks. She has been the recipient of an NEA grant.

John Dorsey is the former poet laureate of Belle, Missouri and the author of *Pocatello Wildflower*. He may be reached at archerevans@yahoo.com.

Gina R. Evers is a poet, educator, and parent. Her work has appeared in *PANK, Quarterly West*, and the *Comstock Review*, among other journals and anthologies. Her writing has been supported by the VCFA Postgraduate Writers' Conference, Martha's Vineyard Institute for Creative Writing, and Lambda Literary Foundation. Gina holds an MFA in creative writing and directs the Mount Saint Mary College Writing Center.

Karen Fabiane: Writing since 1971. Small press publication: *Bound, CAPS 2020, Downtown, Heroin Love Songs, Home Planet News, MisFit, Momoware, New Voices, Newsletter Inago, OM, RagShock* and *Salonika*, among others, plus 5 different Bright Hill Press anthologies. 3 books: *Dancing Bears* (2011), *Seeing You Again* (2014), *Between Canal & Ida* (2022).

Originally from New York in the beautiful Hudson Valley, **Sharon Ferrante** now lives and writes in Daytona Beach, Florida. Her poems have appeared in many anthologies and magazines and journals, including *Rattle, Five Fleas (Itchy Poetry) Scarlet Dragonfly*, and more. Her passion for short form poetry has grown. Much of her work is rooted in myth, whimsy and fancy.

Thomas Festa is a Professor of English at SUNY New Paltz. He is the author of a chapbook of poems, *Earthen* (Finishing Line Press, 2023), and a monograph on John Milton's poetry, *The End of Learning* (Routledge, 2006). Recent publications include poems in *Bennington Review*, *The Briar Cliff Review*, *The Haibun Journal*, and elsewhere.

Mark Fogarty was born in Troy, NY and lives in New Jersey, where he is a former editor of the *Rutherford Red Wheelbarrow*.

Bettina "Poet Gold" Wilkerson offers a soul-searching insight into human existence. Appointed the 2017 and 2018 NYS Dutchess County Poet Laureate, Poet Gold is the recipient of numerous awards. She has spoken at renowned organizations such as The New York State Staff Curriculum Development Network (SCDN) for English Language Arts (ELA). To learn more about "Poet Gold" visit www.poetgold.com

A self educated artist and a world traveler, sculptor, arts educator, poet, painter, and polymath, **Shotsie Gorman's** myriad of creations are currently shown in museums and galleries around the world. He is a globally known tattoo artist and co-founder/former VP of The Alliance of Professional Tattooists. Author of The Black Marks He Made, he often holds poetry and pottery workshops for teens on the edge and County inmates. He is currently traveling coast to coast with an "UNBLOCKING" creativity workshop titled "A Conversation With Shotsie Gorman."

Roberta Gould: Poems published widely: *Confrontation, Mid American, Green Mountain* etc. Anthologies include *Mixed Voices, A Slant of Light, Art/Craft of Poetry*. Translations: Borges, Sor Juana, Pedro Garfias, &others . Latest books: *Talk When You Can,Tell the Truth* (PresaPress), *Woven Lightning*, (SpuytenDuyvil) *Day True* (2023) website: robertagould.net

Carol Graser's work has been published or is forthcoming in many journals, including *Apricity Magazine, The Berkeley Poetry Review, Evening Street Review, Hollins Critic, I-70 Review, The MacGuffin, Midwifery Today, So to Speak, Southern Poetry Review*, and *Home Planet News*. Her collection, *The Wild Twist of Their Stems*, was published by FootHills Publishing in 2007. Since 2003, she's run the monthly poetry series at the legendary Caffe Lena in Saratoga Springs, NY. She has performed her work at various events and venues around New York State.

Meghan Grupposo is a co-founder of NeuroNautic Press. Her publishing credits include *Bouquet* (NeuroNautic Press), & various anthologies, including *NYC From the Inside* (Blue Light Press), *arriving at a shoreline* and *Escape Wheel* (great weather for MEDIA), the *Dada Journal Maintenant*, Issues 14-17 (Three Rooms Press), & *Love Love* Magazine. She holds a BFA in Dance from The Juilliard School.

Maggie Hall is a multidisciplinary artist based in a coastal suburb of Newcastle, NSW Australia. Maggie's studies and writing craft cover all visual art forms within the creative industries; ekphrastic studies; visual translator; use of photography as base across all mediums. She has completed; Bachelor of Fine Art; Master of Creative Industries

Janet Hamill is the author of ten books of poetry and short fiction: *Baby Parade, A Map of the Heavens: Selected Poems 1975-2017, Real Fire, Knock, Tales from the Eternal Café, Body of Water, Lost Ceilings, Nostalgia of the Infinite, The Temple* and *Troublante.* Her poetry has been nominated for the Pushcart Prize and the William Carlos Williams Prize and *Tales from the Eternal Café*, was named one of the "Best Books of 2014" by Publishers Weekly. She's taught at Naropa, Cabrillo College and New England College, where she received her MFA. Recently nominated to the New Milford, NJ Hall of Fame and awarded a commemoration from the State of New Jersey for Outstanding Achievement in the Arts. She is presently at work on her first novel.

Editor for dramatic writing with *The Westchester Review*, poet, playright **Tony Howarth**, retired in 1991 after twenty-eight years as a high school and college teacher of English and theatre. He has served as editor of the editorial page of *The World-Telegram and Sun*. After a 2009 visit to Wordworth's Dove Cottage in England's Lake District he began writing poetry again. His verse dramas *Wild Man of the Mountain* (2021) and *A Hand to Hold* (2022) were published by Broadstone Books.

Dana I. Hunter was one of the Top Ten Poets in the 2021 NAMI NJ: Dara Axelrod Expressive Arts Poetry Contest. She has been published in *Journal of Undiscovered Poets, The Afterpast Review, New Jersey Bards Poetry Review: Anthology 2023, LOVE IN THE ORIGINAL LANGUAGE – ANTHOLOGY, Jerryjazzmusician. com, Mightier—Poets for Social Justice, table/FEAST Literary Magazine,* and *Open Minds Quarterly.*

Matthew Hupert is a writer and multi-media artist from New York City. Matthew hosts several poetry reading series, including the annual showcase for New York voices, *Night in the Naked City*, and the monthly series NeuroNautic Institute Presents, & Don't Bogart that Poem my Friend. He is a recipient of the 2020 New York Acker Award for Show Organizer and Host. He has 2 full length collections, *Ism is a Retrovirus* (2011- Three Rooms Press) and *Secular Pantheism* (2019 - NeuroNautic Press). He is also the author of several chapbooks, & his writing has appeared in numerous journals and anthologies.

Kate Hymes is Ulster County Poet Laureate. She has led Wallkill Valley Writers workshops for over twenty years. Writers, who have written in WVW workshops, have dubbed her the story doula. Her poems have been published in national and regional anthologies. She is currently working on poems inspired by the history of people of African descent in New Paltz and Ulster County.

Sharon Israel's chapbook *Voice Lesson* was published in 2017 (Post Traumatic Press). She won Brooklyn College's Leonard B. Hecht Poetry Explication Award, was nominated for "Best of the Net" and won Four Lines' 2020 winter poetry challenge. Sharon hosts the radio show and podcast, "Planet Poet-Words in Space." https://linktr.ee/sharonisraelpoet.

Kitty Jospé : retired French teacher and Art docent, Kitty has led a weekly poetry appreciation discussion group at two branches of Rochester's library system since February 2008. Started while she was completing her MFA in creative writing at Pacific University (Oregon), the group remains a local highlight. She is a popular reader and speaker, her work appears in many anthologies and publications. Her chapbook, *Mosaicq* was semi-finalist for Finishing Line Press in 2013.

The Gift of Glossophobia [Kelsay Books] is the title of **Mary Louise Kiernan's** debut poetry collection. Her poems appear in numerous print/online journals, with two poems translated into Italian. Twice published in *The New York Times*, she received a 2015 Poetry Prize from Arizona State University. Her website is marylouisekiernan.com.

Ron Kolm is a contributing editor of Sensitive Skin. His books include *A Change in the Weather, Divine Comedy, Duke & Jill, Night Shift, Swimming in the Shallow End* and *The Bookstore Book: A Memoir*. He's had work in The Brownstone Poets anthologies, *The Opiate, Maintenant, The Silver-Tongued Devil anthology, Sparring with Beatnik Ghosts* and *The Café Review*. Ron's papers are archived in the NYU Library.

Susan Konz's work has appeared in *The Waymark* and *CAPS Anthology 2015*. She is a featured contributor to the Calling All Poets Writing Series based in New Paltz, NY. She received her MFA from Hunter College and currently works as an editor for *I Want You to See This Before I Leave*, an online poetry zine. Her first book, *Second Sleep*, was published in 2016 with Lion Autumn Publishing. She is currently working on a new collection.

Darcie Whelan Kortan writes essays (https://darciewk.medium.com and https://literarymama.com/contributor/whelan-kortan-darcie), poems, and blogs. She and her husband have raised boy-girl twins and boy-girl pit bulls in upstate New York, giving her a lifetime of material. On the side, she runs business communications trainings.

Raphael Kosek, an editor at *The Comstock Review*, has published three books: *American Mythology* (Brick Road Poetry Press) and two prize-winning chapbooks, *Harmless Encounters* and *Rough Grace*. She served as the 2019-2020 Dutchess County, NY Poet Laureate where she teaches at Dutchess Community College. www.raphaelkosek.com

Don Krieger is a biomedical researcher whose focus is the electric activity within the brain. Author of the 2020 hybrid collection, *Discovery* (Cyberwit, https://tinyurl.com/2vum5u3u). and 2022's hybrid chapbook, *When Danger Is Past, Who Remembers?* (Milk and Cake Press, https://tinyurl.com/2p8cv95f) He is 2020 Pushcart nominee and a 2020 Creative Nonfiction Foundation Science-as-Story Fellow. His work has appeared in American Journal of Nursing, Neurology, Seneca Review, The Asahi Shimbun, The Blue Nib, The Pittsburgh Post-Gazette, and others, and has been translated into Farsi, Greek, Italian, German, and Turkish.

Katherine Latella's poetry has appeared on the website of Barnard College (her alma mater) as part of their "Pandemic Poets Society" series, and on A Gathering of the Tribes website. She is the Children's Programming Librarian at the Butterfield Library in Cold Spring and lives in Fishkill with her husband.

Bonnie Law has been writing poetry since she was introduced to Emily Dickinson in grade school. She was quoted as saying, "Writing finds me at the oddest places, while driving, in the dentist chair, or sleeping. When it calls, I have no choice but to respond."

Inspired by his friendships with Derek Walcott, Herbert Huncke, and Marty Matz, author, poet, playwright and former background vocalist for New York's underground band Leisure Class, **David Lawton** helps to spirit and maintain great weather for Media and its tireless dedication to published and performed poetry. His collections include *Inspiritive* (Moonstone Press, 2021) and *Sharp Blue Stream* (Three Rooms Press, 2013).

Rain Lee is a sixteen-year-old junior at Haldane High School who writes primarily poetry and fiction, as well as a variety of topics ranging from feminism, family history, dreams, and travelling. She aspires to have her work published professionally and own a private library. She hopes you will enjoy her work.

Phillip X Levine is the poetry editor for Chronogram magazine and president of the Woodstock Poetry Society. His poem, "Rivers & Gardens" was originally conceived in 2002 to present during an event protesting the US invasion of Iraq. Revised, somewhat — sadly, it still seems relevant.

Heller Levinson lives in the lower Hudson Valley. His most recent books are *QUERY CABOODLE & SHIFT GRISTLE* (Black Widow Press, 2023). He won the "2022 Big Other Poetry Award" for *LURK*, (Black Widow Press).

Maria Lisella is the Queens Poet Laureate and an Academy of American Poets fellow. Her work includes *Thieves in the Family* (NYQ Books), and two chapbooks: *Amore on Hope Street* and *Two Naked Feet*. She is poetry editor for VIA, curates the IAWA-NY readings and is a travel writer.

Brian Liston is a life-long Saugerties resident, whose poems have been in *Chronogram*, published in *Riverine: An Anthology of Hudson Valley Writers* as well as his own chapbook, *Through Autistic Eyes*. He also document my life experiences on his blog, The Autistic SuperBlog, which began in 2017 in the hopes to inspire and encourage others who are struggling.

Timothy Liu's latest book of poems is *Down Low and Lowdown: Bedside Bottom-Feeder Blues*. A reader of occult esoterica, he teaches at SUNY New Paltz and Vassar College and lives in Woodstock, NY. www.timothyliu.net

Julie Lomoe received an MFA in painting from Columbia University. Paintings she showed at the 1969 Woodstock Festival are on display at the Bethel Woods Museum. She has published three novels of suspense, all available on Amazon. Her poetry has been featured at many open mics, and her play "Hope Dawns Eternal" was recently featured at Byrdcliffe Theater. Visit her at www.julielomoe.com.

Phil Lynch lives in Dublin, Ireland. His poems have appeared in a range of literary journals and anthologies and his work has been featured on national and local radio in Ireland. His collection, *In a Changing Light*, (Salmon Poetry), was published in 2016.

Writer/actor **Betty MacDonald** has performed her work for WritersRead, TMI Project, and Woodstock Bookfest. Betty hosts Words Carry Us, a monthly livestream of readings and interviews from Green Kill, in Kingston, NY. Her work is included in the anthologies *80 Things to Do When You Turn 80*, *Open House*, *Better With Age*. Her first book of poetry, *All My Monsters are Dead or Why I Love Being Old* (Codhill Press, 2023)

Mary Makofske's latest books are *No Angels* (Kelsay, 2023); *The Gambler's Daughter* (chapbook, Orchard Street Press, 2022); *World Enough, and Time* (Kelsay, 2017); and *Traction* (Ashland Poetry, 2011), winner of the Richard Snyder Prize judged by David Wojahn. Her poems have appeared in 71 journals and in 21 anthologies. www.marymakofske.com

Primarily a songwriter, **John Martucci** presented his first poetry efforts at the Calling All Poets Series (CAPS) and has been writing poems on and off ever since. His poems, like his songs, are short and simple. Published in Waymark and the CAPS 2015 and 2020 Anthologies. A member in good standing at Hudson Valley Haiku Kai with two haiku published in Eastern Structures. Recorded an album of original songs titled "Nothing But a Dream Come True."

Prince McNally is a widely published teaching poet who facilitates workshops through schools & outreach programs, utilizing poetry & creative writing as a means of expression & self-discovery. His work has been nominated for Best of The Net, and the Pushcart Poetry Prize. He resides in Brooklyn NY.

Tana Miller is a member of a long-standing women's writing group, which has published 2 anthologies of their work. The 1st is *An Apple in Her Hand* (Codhill Press; the 2nd is *Rethinking the Ground Rules* (Mediac Books). Her book, *Joseph Cornell: The Man Who Loved Sparrows*, written with co-author Jan Zlotnick Schmidt, will be published by Kelsay Books in 2024.

Ermira Mitre Kokomani is an Albanian, bilingual poet, essayist, and translator living in New Jersey. She has published two poetry collections in Albanian. Her English poetry has appeared in national and international anthologies and magazines. Ermira defines Poetry as the Harp that delivers the Soul's Music. She also translates prose and poetry.

Beth SKMorris, author of: *IN THE AFTERMATH- 9/11 Through a Volunteer's Eyes*, in commemoration of the 20th anniversary; a Pinnacle, Firebird, Book Excellence Award winner, now in the Library of Congress Archive, *The Poetry of 9/11*. Beth holds degrees in English Language & Literature and a Ph.D in Speech, Language, & Hearing Science. She is a member of Hudson Valley Writers Center & Poets House in New York.

K.R. Morrison is a Bay Area poet, drummer, and teen educator who since the pandemic, splits her time between San Francisco and a place she calls Mermaid Town, in Southern California. Morrison is a Pushcart nominee and has featured for several curations and podcasts for her first collection of poetry, *Cauldrons*, published by PaperPress Books.

Karen Neuberg is the author of the full-length poetry collection, *PURSUIT* (Kelsay Press) and the chapbook *the elephants are asking* (Glass Lyre). Her poems have recently appeared in *MAINTENANT 17*, *SurVision*, and *Unbroken*. She is the associate editor of the poetry journal *First Literary Review-East*.

Mary Newell authored the poetry chapbooks *Re-SURGE* and *TILT/ HOVER/ VEER* (Codhill Press), poems in journals and anthologies, and essays including "When Poetry Rivers" (*Interim* journal 38.3). Co-editor of *Poetics for the More-than-Human-World* and the *Routledge Companion to Ecopoetics*, Newell teaches creative writing and Environmental Literature at UConn Stamford. https://manitoulive.wixsite.com/maryn

Perry S. Nicholas is a professor emeritus of English at SUNY at ERIE in Buffalo, N.Y. where he was awarded the SUNY Chancellor's Award and the President's Outstanding Teacher Award. He has published one textbook of poetry prompts, three full-length and seven chapbooks of original poetry, along with two CDs of poetry. You can see his work at perrynicholas.com.

Will Nixon's poetry books include *My Late Mother as a Ruffed Grouse*, *Love in the City of Grudges*, and *Acrostic Woodstock*. With Michael Perkins he co-wrote *Walking Woodstock: Journeys into the Wild Heart of America's Most Famous Small Town*. He also did *The Pocket Guide to Woodstock*.

John Paul O'Connor's poems have appeared in various literary journals, including *Sycamore Review*, *Baltimore Review*, *Columbia Journal of Arts and Literature*, *Indiana Review*, *Seneca Review*, and *Silk Road*. His first book of poems, *Half the Truth*, won the 2015 Violet Reed Haas Prize for Poetry. John lives Franklin, NY.

Irene O'Garden's poetry has reached the Off–Broadway stage (*Women On Fire*), hardcover (*Fat Girl*, *Fulcrum*) paperback (*Risking the Rapids*, *Glad to Be Human*) children's books (*The Scrubbly Bubbly Car Wash*, *Maybe My Baby*) and many literary journals and anthologies. She has received awards, fellowships and residencies for her writing.

Michael Mackin O'Mara, (queer, POZ, poet) works at SoFloPoJo (South Florida Poetry Journal) by day and writes by night. Published in a number of online and print anthologies and journals, their work can be found at www.michaelmackinomara.com @minwpb

Mary K O'Melveny turned to poetry after retiring from a long career as a labor rights lawyer. She lives with her wife near Woodstock, NY. Mary's award-winning poems have appeared in many print and on-line literary journals. She is the author of four poetry collections, including most recently *Flight Patterns*"\ (Kelsay Books 2023) and co-author of two anthologies by the Hudson Valley Women's Writing Group: *Rethinking The Ground Rules* (2022) and *An Apple In Her Hand* (2019).

Kathryn Poppino holds a B.A. in English from Oberlin College and an M.A. in Teaching from SUNY Albany. She is a poet associated with the Washout poetry workshop and has directed several plays for Essex Theatre Company in Essex, NY and serves on its Board of Trustees.

Siobhan Potter lives and works in Ireland. Her practice, centered in relationship explores the capacity of oral poetic form to midwife experience. Siobhan has poems published in print and oral form.

Linette Rabsatt is a Virgin Islander who recently published a Kindle book, *Be Inspired: Poems by Linette Rabsatt*. You can also find my work in *Virgin Islands Callaloo: Poems from the Caribbean* and on the Visual Verse website. In addition, I share some pieces in Virgin Islands newspapers and on my blog, Words of Ribbon.

Carrie Magness Radna is a Special Collections cataloger at NYPL, a singer and a poet. She is an Associate Editor of *Brownstone Poets Anthology* (2022-2023) and was recently nominated for Best of the Web. Her book *Shooting Myself in the Dark*, was published by Cajun Mutt Press in January 2023.

Suzanne S. Rancourt, an award winning, internationally published author of four books: *Songs of Archilochus*, Unsolicited Press, 2023; *Old Stones, New Roads*, MSR Pub., 2021, *murmurs at the gate*, Unsolicited Press, 2019; *Billboard in the Clouds*, Curbstone Press, 2004 2nd print NU Press. She is a USMC and Army Veteran.

Guy Reed won the 2022 Littoral Press poetry prize and is author of *Second Innocence* (Luchador Press), *The Effort To Hold Light* (Finishing Line Press), and co-author, with Cheryl A. Rice, of *Until The Words Came* (Post Traumatic Press). From Minnesota, Guy now resides in the Catskills Mountains. <guyedwinreed.com>

Liz Reilly resides in the Lower Hudson Valley in New York State. Her poetry explores themes of love, grief, the process of writing, and pagan spirituality. She is also a crafter, focused primarily on the fiber arts. She can also be found at local and online poetry readings and workshops.

Sally Rhoades, a choreographer, writer, director, poet, and performer, has presented work across the U.S. and in Canada. She was born in Malone, N.Y. She received her MA in Creative writing at the University of Albany in Albany, NY, where she studied women's contemporary poetry, playwriting, directing and performance. She lives in Albany, N.Y.

Twice a Best of the Net nominee, **Cheryl A. Rice's** books include *Dressing for the Unbearable* (Flying Monkey Press), *Until the Words Came* (Post Traumatic Press), and *Love's Compass* (Kung Fu Treachery Press). Her monthly column, The Flying Monkey, is at https://hvwg.org/, while her occasional blog is at http://flying-monkeyprods.blogspot.com/. Rice can be reached at dorothyy62@yahoo.com.

Stephen Thomas Roberts (he, his, him) is a retired lawyer currently pursuing an MFA in Creative Writing (Poetry) from Sarah Lawrence College. He resides in Dutchess County. Mr. Roberts's work has appeared in many journals, including *Gargoyle, Poetry Salzburg Review, The Haibun Journal,* and *The Worcester Review.*

Tom Romeo has been writing and performing his poetry and stories for nearly thirty years. A member of the Long Island Poetry Society and The Performing Poets Association, he moved to Kingston, NY in 2014 and has performed all over the Hudson Valley. His work can be found in four chapbooks: *Remember?, Demented Love, OMG,* and *Good Mourning: Loving Robin Romeo*. A collection of videos of his performances can be found at www.whereforearts.com. He can be reached at tom@tomromeo.com

Amanda Russell (she/her/hers) is a guest editor at *The Comstock Review* and a stay-at-home mom. Her poems have appeared in *Hole in the Head re:View, EcoTheo Review, Lily Poetry Review,* and *Open: a Journal of Arts and Letters*. To learn about her or her chapbook, Barren Years, please visit https://poetrussell.wordpress.com/.

Award-winning poet, interdisciplinary artist, and cultural worker **Stephanie JT Russell's** poetry has appeared in numerous books and journals and at noted art and performance venues. Appointed Dutchess County Poet Laureate 2023, Russell is curating "Stream of Life," a series of multidisciplinary events from diverse Hudson Valley communities. https://www.artsmidhudson.org/dc-poetlaureate / www.stephaniejtrussell.com

Margaret R. Sáraco began writing about feminism and music. She has been nominated for a Pushcart Prize and twice recognized in the Allen Ginsberg Poetry Contest. Her poetry collections *If There Is No Wind* (2022) and *Even the Dog Was Quiet* (2023) were both published with Human Error Publishing.

Teaching undergraduate courses in literature, composition, and creative writing at Marist College, **Judith Saunders** has lived and worked in the Mid-Hudson Valley for many years. Her poetry has appeared in a wide variety of periodicals and anthologies, both regional and national in scope, including *Chronogram, Oxalis, Blueline, Chiron Review, Poet Lore, South Carolina Review, ISLE, Folio, California Quarterly, Christian Science Monitor, Concho River Review, Soundings East,* and elsewhere. She is the author of two prize-winning chapbook collections of poetry (*Panhandler, Red Berry*).

Jan Zlotnik Schmidt's work has been published in many journals including *Kansas Quarterly, The Alaska Quarterly Review*. Her poetry volumes include *We Speak in Tongues; She had this memory* (the Edwin Mellen Press) and *Foraging for Light* (Finishing Line Press). Her poetry has been nominated for the Pushcart Press Prize.

Moe Seager arranges, phrases and drops syllables in jazz time. Spoken word and in song, Moe renders by voice as instrument. Seager has published seven collections and three jazz poetry albums. Translated-published in French, Italian and Arabic. Currently with Camion press, Milan. From Paris he skipped town from Pittsburgh and the NYC upper west side. Contact Moe Seager @ Fb, YouTube, Fb Angora Poets World Café.

William Seaton is a poet, translator, and critic who read with Jim Eve and Mike Jurkovic even before Calling All Poets, which they and their colleagues have developed into the region's premiere poetry series. Seaton is the author of *Spoor of Desire: Selected Poems* and *Dada Poetry: An Introduction* and has been active in poetry performance since the sixties. He maintains a largely literary blog at williamseaton.blogspot.com.

Jim Seegert's been a reader and feature throughout metro NYC with the Performance Poets Association, The Phoenix Reading Series and Fahrenheit 100. He's been published in *PPA Literary Reviews, the Tamarind Review, Verse-Virtual* and aired on WRHU (Hofstra University) radio. He reads monthly at Lit Lit, (Beacon, NY), and at CAPs.

Debbie Shave is a writer of science-fiction, fantasy, poetry and humorous essays. She has been published in various print and online magazines and is a member of the Hudson Valley writers' group, Wild Plums.

Nancy Shih-Knodel is author of the chapbook, *The Landscape of the Body* (Red Bird Chapbooks, 2016), and her poems have been published in the *Crab Orchard Review, Water-Stone Review, The Examined Life Journal, Martin Lake Journal, Third Wednesday, Midway Journal,* and *The Heartland Review*. She has also been nominated for "Best of the Net." She currently lives in Hopewell Junction, New York.

Gary Siegel: I am a Poet. My writing is driven by journeys into nature as well as the inner journeys. When I found the CAPS, I found an environment. I would say that at CAPs – we take our poetry seriously, but not necessarily ourselves. There is the feeling that the readers here are deeply dug into their craft, while all are welcome and encouraged to work their art. The place has that feel. After a night at CAPS I want to love reading more and I want to get better. I also want very much to come back.

Nathan Smith is a 25-year old poet and author of *Cotton Candy Sun* from Lewis Run, Pennsylvania. These days he is working on his PhD in Biochemistry and Biophysics from RPI and residing in Troy NY. You can find him on instagram @cottoncandypoems or at local open mics trying out new work.

Megha Sood is an Award-winning Asian-American Poet, Editor, and Literary Activist. A Literary Partner with "Life in Quarantine", at Stanford University. Her edited anthology and poetry have been selected as a digital payload to be sent to the moon in 2024 in collaboration with NASA/SpaceX. Link: https://linktr.ee/meghasood

My name is **Amanda Spadafino**, and I still don't know what that means. What I can tell you is that as lost as I am in my mind, the strongest foundation I have is in my heart. And for every time I've lost my words, I've found them in writing just the same. My poetry is the most naked form of how I can understand what it means to be human in the most complex and simple of ways. So if there's anything I can confidently tell you about myself, it wouldn't be much more than my name and my poetry – but I'm okay with that.

Matthew J. Spireng's 2019 Sinclair Poetry Prize-winning book *Good Work* was published by Evening Street Press. An 11-time Pushcart Prize nominee, he is the author of two other full-length poetry books, *What Focus Is* and *Out of Body*, winner of the 2004 Bluestem Poetry Award, and five chapbooks.

Lisa St. John is a writer living in upstate New York. She is the author of *Ponderings* (Finishing Line Press) and *Swallowing Stones* (Kelsay Books). Lisa's poetry appears in journals such as *New Verse News*, *The Poet's Billow*, *The Orchards Poetry Journal*, *Light*, *Poets Reading the News*, and *Glassworks*.

Jeffrey Stubits: I'm an Albany poet, theater actor, videographer, and mushroom forager. I enjoy swimming, baseball, yoga, and martial arts. I took in a stray cat about three weeks ago. I didn't know she was pregnant at the time. And now, my life will never be the same...

Victoria Sullivan is both a poet and a playwright, a member of the Woodstock Fringe Playwrights Unit and of the American Renaissance Theatre Company, and performs her poetry with jazz musicians locally in the Hudson Valley. She is the "poet laureate" of the Woodstock Roundtable on WDST 100.1 FM.

Tim Tomlinson's books include *Requiem for the Tree Fort I Set on Fire* (poetry), and *This Is Not Happening to You* (fiction). *Listening to Fish: meditations from the wet world*, appears with Nirala Publishing in 2024. Tim is the director of New York Writers Workshop. He teaches in NYU's Global Liberal Studies.

Daniel Villegas is a Spoken Word and Bilingual Emcee from Colombia based in the United States. His set references the Latin American experience/Hispanic culture. Daniel Villegas goes from poem to poem with the use of rhyme expressing the importance of self knowledge and expression. He will also be playing the conga tying in the history from *Africa to the Diaspora of the Indigenious and Spanish influences.*

George Wallace is writer in residence at the Walt Whitman Birthplace, editor of *Poetrybay* and co-editor of *Great Weather for Media*, author of 40 chapbooks of poetry, creator of 4 albums of spoken word poetry/music, and a NYC-based poet who travels internationally to share his work.

Bruce Weber is the author of six books of poems, most recently THERE ARE TOO MANY WORDS IN MY HOUSE (Rogues Scholars Press, 2019).

Glenn Werner: Graphic Designer for fifty years, Poet for about twenty five. A self published book, a few chapbooks. Formerly Vice President of CAPS. Retired from all of that. Working on art that may pull it together. Busy sorting through the playing pieces I've collected. Seeing what I can make of it.

Although **Dan Wilcox** once worked as a dishwasher & as a short-order cook, he has never driven a cab. For most of his career he worked as a bureaucrat & wrote poetry. He was named one of the 2019 Literary Legends by the Friends and Foundation of the Albany Public Library. He claims to have "the World's largest collection of photos of unknown poets." He is the host of the Third Thursday Poetry Night at the Social Justice Center in Albany, NY & is an active member of Veterans For Peace.

Sandy Yannone (2nd place) (she/her/they/them), *Boats for Women* (Salmon Poetry 2019) & *The Glass Studio* (Salmon 2024), host of Cultivating Voices LIVE Poetry, Sundays on Facebook via Zoom, co-host of West-East Bicoastal Poets of the Pandemic and Beyond. Board member, Olympia Poetry Network—to learn more, please visit my website at www.sandrayannone.com

Many Special Thanks

When we decided to create and publish a 25th Anniversary Anthology, we knew immediately we would have to include those special friends who stood alongside of us at the CAPS' podium for a while and moved on. It is only inevitable that we overlooked one or two.

With that said, our In Memoriam section would not have been possible without the work, words, and yes love of the following:

Poems and bio of Pauline Uchmanowicz courtesy of and special thanks to Joann Deiudicibus.

Poems and bio of Saul Bennett courtesy of and special thanks to Will Nixon.

Poems and bios of Barbara Boncek, Enid Dame, Lei Isaacs, Shirley Powell, Janine Pommy-Vega, and Ralph Villano courtesy of and special thanks to Cheryl A Rice.

Poems, bio, and photo of Bob Barci courtesy of and special thanks to Mark Lichtenstein.

Previously unpublished poems of Donald Lev courtesy of and special thanks to Phillip Levine.

Poems of Ron Whiteurs courtesy of and special thanks to Mikhail Horowitz.

Special thanks to Dan Wilcox for his photos of Saul Bennett, Frank Boyer, Enid Dame, Donald Lev, Shirley Powell, Janine Pommy Vega, Ron Whiteurs, and Don Yacullo.

Special thanks to Christopher Wheeling for his photos of Donald Lev, Lynn Hoins, Pamela Twining, and Ron Whiteurs.

A special thanks to the words and spirit of Steve Dalachinsky (1946-2019).

Special mention also to Bill Keith (1929–2004) who was there in Beacon when this whole journey started.

CAPS Board

Published globally with little reportable income, **Mike Jurkovic's** full lengths include *Buckshot Reckoning, mooncussers, AmericanMental*, (Luchador Press 2023, 2022, 2020). *Blue Fan Whirring* (Nirala Press, 2018) 2016 Pushcart nominee. President Calling All Poets. Co-chairs Rosendale Theatre Music Fan Film Series. Reviews appear at All About Jazz & lightwoodpress.com Hosts New Jazz Excursions, Mondays, 9-10am, WVKR-91.3FM Vassar College. The Rock n Roll Curmudgeon appeared in Rhythm and News Magazine, 1996-2003. He loves Emily most of all.

6 Haiku

in the zen of a
sudden flurry my wild grapes
too tart for the wine

a tethered solo
leaves me downhearted unsure
of the steps ahead

the long pursuit of
acceptance   exhausts the mind
walks the days sadly

the year   exhausted
my bones older my heart just
barely   holding on

in my dream without
oars there was no dry land no
raft just days of rain

I will go as far
and fall wherever God's cool
wind delivers me

Jim Eve is the originator of the Calling All Poets Inc. Calling All Poets was a program that originated at the Howland Cultural Center when Jim was a board member there back in 1999. Along the way he partnered with Mike Jurkovic and together with the help of long time supporters move the program forward. The program obtained its own non-profit status in June of 2014. Jim, who writes poetry whenever the mood strikes him, considers himself more of a facilitator of poetry than a poet.

Whatever Happened to Leo

Whatever happened to Leo
A white man pale and frail
Black yarmulke on his head
A bodega owner who prevailed.

He lived amongst us Blacks and Latinos
Spoke English, Spanish even Ladino.
Sold us groceries Leo did
Gave out rock candy to the neighborhood kids.

A 174th Street Jew
a man of easy speaking
A white light in a dark Bronx
Which wasn't easy keeping.

Whatever happened to Leo?
I surely wish I knew
He was certainty one lone dumpling
In a pot of Southern Boulevard stew!

Ken Holland: When I recently featured, I shared that CAPS is my poetic home. And how when I judge certain poems to be worthy enough, I keep on ice until I have the chance to give them their first airing in New Paltz. The steady caliber of work presented at the monthly readings is the best in the valley. If this sounds more like a biography of CAPS than myself, that's wholly appropriate.

Punchline

A priest
an Israeli soldier
and a Hamas fighter
walk into a bar.

That's where the joke ends.

So stop laughing.

Greg Correll, CAPS Board member, was a Fellow at the CUNY Writers Institute in 2017, where he worked closely with Leo Carey (*The New Yorker*) and Jonathan Galassi (*FSG*). Wrote about his Parkinson's diagnosis (Salon), and sexual assaults in jail at 14 (Medium). In a half-dozen essay/poetry anthologies, including *Into Sanity* (2019), co-edited by Mark Vonnegut. Two short plays produced, one off-Broadway. A freelance editor, he loves helping writers improve and polish. Three ferocious, brilliant daughters.

Your Mouth

Pursed as you measure, soundless as you read along.
The ache of tarry a while, of longing, as I watch you make
each dish, an affirmation in fingertips folding, pinching.
Trusting recipes the way cousins trust psalms:
prepare and assemble, mix and stir—your mouth
in movement over the meal, your daven involuntary,
full of fragmentary satisfactions, alert motions.
Your palms hover over bowl and skillet and board.
As I watch your tiny smiles they blur, turn gold.
I cry a little and bite my whiskey'd maraschino.

25TH ANNIVERSARY